Double
or Quits

To Jill, my mother Nancy, my children, Kieran,
Tristan and Tahli and to John and Matthew
Hayes for their support and encouragement.

Published by bigbluetube, Liverpool
Book design by March Design, Liverpool
Cover design Juice Creative Design Ltd, Leicester
Printed in the United Kingdom by Henry Ling Limited, at the
Dorset Press, Dorchester, DT1 1HD

Thanks to everyone who has supplied photographs, including: Michael
Stockton Photography, Target Studios, The Daily Mirror, The Leicester
Mercury, Neville Chadwick Photography and David Muscroft Photography.

ISBN 0 9545841 1 2

Double or Quits

Willie Thorne
with Derek Marsden

www.**big**blue**tube**.com

FOREWORD

I've known Willie Thorne all my adult life. We have shared each other's triumphs and experiences. We have supported each other as we were developing as professional sportsmen. More importantly, we have also given each other the support that springs naturally from friendship in trying times when you need it the most.

We are both from Leicester and both still have strong links with the city. Willie is based in the area and, as a well known moustache-grower and smooth talker, he has been in demand for a whole clutch of local charities. He keeps this side of his life private but there is no disputing the fact that he has helped raise an enormous amount of money, especially for children's charities.

An involvement in so many charity ventures comes naturally to someone like Willie. He has that gift of sociability and an ease of communicating with so many different types of people.

He has told me for 25 years that he is the greatest player *never* to have won the Embassy World Championship. He always looked good when he was playing against me, but then I've got an even bigger box of excuses than Willie. His generosity of spirit knows no bounds as he showed, time after time, in pushing me to my title of 'Snooker Player with the Most 147s Scored Against Him'. Thanks Willie.

Willie has had his hard times over the last few years and I can only admire his bravery in being so honest and open about his problems in the pages of this book. It is difficult for a sportsman to adapt to his new life after his playing days are over and it is great to see Willie throwing himself into so many new ventures using and developing his talent as a communicator and as a commentator. Who knows where he will end up? ... Talk show host, panelist, anchorman. Whatever he tries, I'm sure he will give it the Maximum ...

Gary Lineker

chapter one
SICK AS A PARROTT

This was like a play somebody had written for me. I was in Scotland. I was still Willie Thorne, the snooker player, but my career was fading and my debts were mounting. I wasn't playing in the Regal Masters at the Motherwell Civic Centre but I had been invited by BBC Scotland to come up and commentate on the tournament with my old friends Dennis Taylor and Phil Yates.

I always drove to Scotland for tournaments and exhibitions. It was only a four hour drive but, on that September day in 1996, it felt like a lifetime. I had played the previous year in this invitational event but this time I'd been passed over. That hurt, but I was starting to get used to the occasional rejection.

By the time I arrived at the hotel in Motherwell, after all those hours in my own company, I was really down. During the drive, I'd gone over in my mind all the details of my gambling debts. After more than 15 years as a big earning professional, I'd built up a large portfolio of accounts with various bookmakers. My status and earning power had made it easy for me to open up lots of accounts with access to huge amounts of credit but now I was building up thousands of pounds of debt with four or five bookmakers.

Dennis Taylor was at the hotel when I arrived and, as we'd done so many times before all over the world, we went off to have meal together. There was a Chinese restaurant close to the hotel which we'd used the previous year and, by now, I'd snapped back into my Willie Thorne persona, having a chat and a bit of a laugh with one of my best friends in the game.

Just as we were finishing our meal, in walked John Parrott to get a takeaway. JP was not his usual happy self, understandably, as it turned out.

"I've just come from Heathrow," said John glumly. "My car's been broken into at the airport and my cue's been nicked. I've got a new one but I'm playing awful. I've only had it a day and I just can't get it right."

We sympathised, naturally, as you would with anybody who has had property stolen, but we realised, as fellow pros, just how serious this was. A snooker player can take up to two months to get used to a new cue and that could mean a string of defeats and a slip down the rankings. John was well aware of my gambling and came out with the killer phrase – "Willie, don't back me tomorrow". My mind went into overdrive and pound signs rolled around in my eyes. This was it! You may think me callous but all I could think of was that there was no way I could lose, betting against John. This could be the end of my problems – again!

We went back to the hotel. It was late but we both had some serious phone calls to make. Dennis is not a gambler: he'd go into a casino perhaps every six months and be prepared to lose a couple of hundred quid. On the way back from the restaurant Dennis couldn't shut me up as I went on and on about the gift horse called Parrott that had just walked into our lives. This was such a certainty, I told him, that it would be stupid not to make a little killing out of our inside knowledge. After ten minutes of badgering, I'd convinced him to bet as much as he could on the match and so off he went to phone his son in Blackburn to tell him to put £500 on Ken Doherty, JP's opponent. Meanwhile, I was starting to go through my list of contacts.

The first person I phoned was 'Racing' Raymond, my old mate from Leicester and asked him to put £5,000 on Doherty for me. I told him the story and he didn't hesitate to give me a guarantee. My mind was racing by now. I was racking my brains trying to think of everybody I'd been on betting expeditions with.

I next phoned two more of my gambling pals, Micky Fletcher and Nigel Trough, followed by a few others before I went to bed. It was important to spread the betting around the country in small lots, to as many bookmakers as possible, before anyone realised there was a coup in the air. This was the normal practice when somebody in our circle heard about an absolute certainty. I was so excited for myself and for all my mates, as here had come one of those wondrous, rare moments – the realisation that you had a cast iron certainty and that you were bound to beat the bookmaking system.

I went up to bed and, unsurprisingly, sleep was impossible. My

Dennis Taylor has been a great friend from our early days as professionals.

mind was racing through all the things I would have to do before the bookies opened at 9.30am. I still had more phone calls to make to my network of contacts.

I started phoning really early, apologising to everybody about ruining their lie-in but convincing them that there was easy money to be earned that day. I must have sounded really manic, completely unable to contain my joy. I managed over 20 calls before ten o'clock, by which time I had been able to get people to stake £38,000 on a Doherty victory. I told everybody to put a couple of grand on for themselves and another thousand for me. There is always the danger that when you contact people this way the news will spread like wild fire and betting will be suspended too early, leaving you with a pittance. I was lucky to have put so much on before the suspension came at 10.30 that morning, when the strange betting pattern was finally picked up by the bookmaking fraternity. We'd managed to put a lot of money on at 6/5, although by 10.30 it had gone down to 4/7, or as John McCirrick would call it, a flip flop favourite. Nonetheless, despite these low odds, I was expecting a tidy windfall of about £35,000 by the end of the day.

As the morning wore on, I grew more and more tense. I was on a high, unlike John Parrott certainly who'd given interviews to local radio and television telling the world about his stolen cue and advising any punters not to back him but that, of course, was impossible by then anyway.

The first four-frame session was due to start at 1.30pm. Happy as a sand-boy as I almost skipped into the commentary box with Phil. I tried hard to keep my smug glow under control, as well as my mouth, as Doherty took the first frame without too much bother. "John is shaking his head," I commented. "He looks as if the world's troubles are on his shoulders." There were hardly any on mine.

By now, Phil was having a real problem getting a word in edgeways and calming me down and all those critics who say I talk too much, were having a field day. I thought I'd better start making excuses for JP, reminding the viewers of the story of the lost cue. He was making mistake after mistake and the second frame was lost as he missed two easy chances to win. He couldn't pot a ball and so Doherty tidied up the frame. I was grinning even more broadly than I normally do. I kept thinking, "£35,000 – that'll ease the pain. I'll settle a few accounts and then have a nice lump sum to start recouping my losses."

Ken won that second frame after making a 70 break and, according to my comments from the box, he only had to stand up to win. Then, totally unexpectedly, John started to rally and made a couple of 20 breaks, managing to nick the next two frames. So the interval came with the score 2-2, and Willie Thorne hanging on to the edge of cloud nine by his fingernails.

The interval lasted 50 minutes, allowing me enough time to make a few reassuring phone calls to Racing Raymond and the others. My name was heading for the mud bath and I could just imagine them all tearing their hair out, watching the score coming in on Ceefax. "Don't worry, lads. Parrott should be four nil down. He can't pot a ball."

Then I bumped into John who was wearing that JP glum trademark expression, "I'm trying my hardest, but what can I do with that plank?"

The afternoon session continued, with John playing some very unconvincing snooker but scratching his way through a few short, two-colour breaks. Unbelievably, the fifth frame went to him and, before I knew it, he had chalked up the next two, although still without making a 50 break. So it was 5-2.

Perhaps JP thought at this stage that he had a real chance of winning, as he now relaxed his grip. Doherty won the eighth frame and I saw a chink of light, although I was still bathed in sweat and my stomach was churning.

As the last frame wound on, I was convinced that Fate had it in for me. It was the hardest commentating job I've ever done but I still kept putting out the standard waffle. "John Parrott hasn't played well but he's buckled down, used his experience and played some gutsy snooker... "

So the inevitable happened – Parrott won the ninth frame and the match – he did it without making a single break of 50. I still can't believe it. If they'd played ten matches against each other straight after, Ken Doherty would have won the lot. It was a fluke that happens now and again and a result that John Parrott and I have laughed about for years afterwards.

I was left with a week's commentary still to do. I was absolutely skint. All my available cash had gone on the bet. Bankruptcy was now looming very large on the horizon and I realised I was back on the same slippery slope I had gone down in the 80s.

Photographs from the
family album.

Above, at the seaside
with Dad.

chapter two
LITTLE WILLIE

So how had I got into this mess? How had gambling crept up on me again and again and virtually ruined my life?

When I look back on my life, it is easy now for me to see the germination of the gambling bug, though it seems barely credible to me as I flick through the photos and mental pages of my childhood. I didn't come from a gambling background, although my mother was one of a handful of people who backed Foinavon at 100/1 to win the 1967 Grand National. My father, too, was never a bad role model as I was growing up. He would gamble occasionally but that did not happen until I was in my teens. Usually, it was only when he went racing, and a flutter is an essential part of the day out, so I could not, in real honesty, put any of the blame on Dad.

There were no obvious bad influences in my childhood in Anstey Village just to the west of Leicester. I was born there in March 1954, in the neat semi that was to be my home until my early teens. It was basically a commuter settlement for Leicester, though my father travelled in the opposite direction away from the city to Desford colliery, where he worked as a miner. Those people who know me as Willie Thorne, son of a miner, have this crazy notion that Anstey was an archetypal mining village and that I was some kind of working class hero who had hacked his way out of it. We didn't keep pigeons and we didn't have a whippet. Shame really, it would make a better beginning to the Willie Thorne Story.

Anstey was, in fact, a very ordinary village on the edge of a city with its own pubs, schools and a few small businesses. It was the kind of place in which footballers lived before the gold rush of the 1990s. Just to underline that point, Derek Dougan, Leicester City's centre forward in the late 60s was our next door neighbour for a couple of years. Being on the edge of open countryside, I was always aware of the rural spaces around us.

Like many of people in the area, we were into shooting and I remember so clearly leaning out of my bedroom window and taking shots at rabbits in the neighbouring field. There was a time when I hit one and then watched it crawl under a hedge. I dashed out of the house to try to fish it out but the Avenging Angel must have been watching and I ended up in hospital with a badly gashed hand. My dad used to take me shooting rabbits in my early teens at Gorse Hill every Saturday morning. These, I suppose, were our bonding sessions. He would offer me a Newcastle Brown and encourage me to smoke, but I rejected these two of my father's vices and stayed that way throughout my life.

Anstey was big enough to have a number of primary schools and a large middle school. I have a few vague memories of my time at Anstey Martin Primary. Certainly nothing momentous happened that was to shape my future. However, when I transferred from the infants to the juniors, I began to develop a keen interest in sport.

People who have gone on to make their living as professional sportsmen always remember their sports teachers and I'm no exception. I became close to Dave Geary and George Kershaw who looked after the school's football and cricket teams and helped me develop my sporting ability. They didn't teach me a thing about snooker but they did build up my interest in sport, and with it, my self-confidence.

I was a pretty good centre forward in those days. I was tall and, as you can see from the old photos, I had a big quiff and a full head of hair – later to be replaced with a full head of skin! My friends played in the team with me. It's a long time ago, but I can still remember lads like Bob May, Martin Gibbons, Chris Hackett and Chris Bird. We used to go to each others' houses, play football on the Anstey Nomads' training pitch and practise cricket on the driveway of our house. In other words, we had the kind of life enjoyed by so many English kids in the 1960s.

We have drifted apart over the years but it's nice to reflect on those days and wonder what happened to those lads. I know through the grapevine that two of the group are now dead: one was killed in a car crash, the other died from a stroke. I may sound maudlin but it does make you think about your own mortality and good fortune when you look back at your past.

I was a pretty good centre forward. I'm second left in the front row of our school team.

Whether it was those practice sessions, or the inspiration of my teachers, or the example of my older brother, my cricket improved throughout my teens. Eventually, I made it into the Cropston village team and then into the Leicestershire Colts side. I probably could have played cricket at a very good level but I was never to know because events conspired to throw me into the game that was to become my obsession – snooker.

When you look back on your life you often wonder how things would have turned out if certain fairly minor events had not happened. I cannot remember why my brother, Malcolm, asked for and was given a 6ft x 3ft snooker table for a Christmas present, but its arrival changed the direction of my life. I was soon playing on it at every available opportunity as my obsession with the game took hold.

That same year we went on holiday to Eastbourne and stayed at the York Hotel, where I came across the first full-sized table on which I was allowed to play. My mother, as a sharp contrast to Woody Allen's mother, has always put me on a pedestal instead of under it. She wrote years later to the hotel telling them that they should realise that Willie Thorne, professional snooker player, had his first game on a proper table at their hotel. I'm not sure whether they were impressed.

It was pretty obvious by now that I had some ability playing snooker and so my mother bought me my first snooker cue for my 14th birthday. She went to a sport's shop in Leicester and bought me the best cue they had, a Walter Lindrum Maple model which cost £3.2s.6p. Thirty-six years later I am still using it. I have had adaptations made over the years and it is now a two piece cue but it still has the original butt and shaft. It was so important to me and my self-confidence during my playing career, that I would have given at least £10,000 for its return if ever it had been stolen. I have made every one of my maximum 147 breaks with that cue and, I suppose, transferred some of these insecurities to John Parrott on that fateful meeting in a Chinese restaurant in Motherwell.

Perhaps the most important 'minor' event that was to shape my life in those days, was the closure of Desford Colliery. My dad was made redundant and was briefly unemployed until he took what he thought was going to be a stop-gap job. The chairman of Anstey Conservative Club, Howard Brangley, worked with my mother at Airborne Shoes in Anstey. He was a family friend and was able to pull a few strings to get my dad a job as a steward of the club. He was well suited to the job as he was very big and brash and also very personable. Crucially, as it turned out, the club had a snooker table and I was able to play on it regularly. Thank god, looking back, it didn't have a table tennis table.

I made rapid progress as I became more and more obsessed by the game. I was playing with the club members whenever they'd let me. One of them was Joe Young, a Geordie who'd moved down to Leicester and who became my first coach. He was a good amateur player and certainly the best at the Conservative Club. His coaching was very informal, just a few words here or there during the course of the game. He had a lovely cue action, always striking the ball clearly before going off to pick up a cigarette, or have another long draw on his pipe.

Although a lot of the members by now were quite keen to play with me, or be part of the crowd that wanted to watch me, a complaint was made to the committee about me monopolising the club's single table. In the end, a compromise was reached and they decided to allow me to play between 11am and noon and in the evening between 5pm and 6pm. These were the quiet times at the club, so I was able to play six or seven frames a day without annoying anybody. Without those first few years when Dad was at the club, who knows how differently my life would have turned out.

Dad, by now, had learnt how to run a social club, so he went for the next step – the licensed trade. He took on the tenancy of the Shoulder of Mutton, an Everard's pub in the Braunston area of Leicester. It was a massive pub in the middle of a council estate and had the reputation of being a difficult tenancy. My parents threw all their energy into running the pub, my mother giving up her job at Airborne and the family moving into the tenant's flat above the pub. As luck would have it, there was also a large empty store room in the premises. I'd left school by this stage and with my earnings from the glass company for which I worked, I managed to buy a table for 50 quid. Inevitably, the purchase was subsidised by my parents, who were starting to earn a bob or two from all the long hours they were putting in at the pub. Now I was able to practise at every available opportunity, encouraged by both Mum and Dad.

Soon after leaving school, I had become so good at snooker that I became the National Under-16 Snooker Champion, after less than two years playing the game and I was starting to come into contact with a whole new world – a world that would shape the rest of my life.

On the table at the
Shoulder of Mutton.

chapter three

OSBORNE'S

As I neared the end of my time at school, I started to move into an arena which was to raise my standard of snooker but also where gambling was part and parcel of everyday life. In the centre of Leicester, not far from the market, was a place built rather like an aircraft hangar. This was Osborne's Billiard Hall, so typical of those establishments in the 1960s. It was, in lots of ways, a spit and sawdust place, always busy, full of people from the market. It was very basic with just a small tea room next to the tiny office of Mr and Mrs Osborne, the owners. It was the kind of institution you found in every city, where there was always somebody drifting in selling radios, TVs etc. It was also a club where a lot of wagers were being made on the games and where gossip was exchanged about the horses that were running that day all over the country.

I had started out as just a 15-year-old who took his 2s.6d pocket money down to the club every Saturday for the junior session while my mum went shopping in Leicester city centre. To begin with, I would lose straightaway to players who were better than me. This meant that my bus fare was gone and the four mile journey back to Anstey was often on foot. I had only been playing for a year but I was determined to improve and save that long walk with my new cue inside its golden case. I must have looked like a proper prat, a real jack the lad, but I kept at it and, within six months, my game had improved to such an extent that, by the age of 16, I was beating the likes of Brian Cakebread, the best player in the city.

I was coming into contact with good players outside the small pond of Leicester snooker as I began to enter national championships. I met Joe Johnson and Tony Knowles for the first time at the UK Junior Championships in Birmingham, and I began to realise the way my life was taking me. I had grown used to playing for side bets and Joe was a bit taken aback when I suggested playing in practice for a fiver instead of the five bob he was used to.

As I said, by this time I'd left school and was working for a glass merchants in Leicester. I used to go down to Osborne's every lunchtime from work and, by this stage, my reputation had grown so much that there would often be up to 30 people gathering around table 14 to watch a 16-year-old take on the best in the club. There were 22 tables in the club, all of them kept immaculately clean by Ernie Osborne, but he reserved the best for me, as I was bringing lots of custom in those dinner hour sessions.

Breaking the 100 break barrier was a defining moment. I probably made ten breaks in the 90s before I broke through with a 109 at Osborne's one lunch hour. After that, it was as if a psychological dam had been broken and I made dozens of them.

I must have played 350 challenge matches in Osborne's over the following five years. I was picking up more and more money from side bets but I was only really interested in playing and winning. My headmaster's remark on a school report was still in my head. 'He will never make a living playing snooker. He must try harder.' Nevertheless, the money started building up. I was still working for Eden's as an estimator, which meant I was travelling around from job to job and was virtually my own boss. I was finishing jobs quickly to make time to get down to Osborne's for lunch time and afternoon sessions, winning more often than losing.

By the time I was 18, I was earning enough money to give in my notice to Barry Eden. I had enjoyed working for him but knew when it was time to go, even though the idea of turning professional was still not in my mind. In the early 70s, there was still very little money in the game and very little coverage in the press or on television. When Higgins won the Embassy World Championship in 1972 only the highlights of the final were shown on Grandstand one Saturday afternoon.

However, the amateur game could be quite lucrative, mainly through gambling and wagers. When I was 18, I'd won £500 and used it to buy my first Ford Escort. This was quickly followed by a Cortina MKII bought for £2,000 after a big win in North Ormesby. I'd been invited to play in a tournament at the Institute in the town where first prize money of £400 was up for grabs. I put £200 on myself for the first round and then reinvested all the way to the

The Standard Triumph team won the CIU Club Championship three years in a row. Brian Cakebread is holding the trophy.

Showing off my trophies.

final, ending up £4,000 in credit. I was so exhilarated winning so much in one tournament, in the days when the average annual salary was only just over £1,000. I took the car out for a spin the day after I bought it and drove it into a ditch while I was only doing 30mph. I wasn't a crap driver, I was just in love with all the fancy dials on the dashboard.

After winning the Under-19 Championship again, the next step was to be chosen as the youngest competitor ever to play for my country. There was no money in this at all, though we were paid hotel and travel expenses. Matches were at weekends and we travelled to most of the venues by coach. Mark Wildman usually sat next to me and he'd be easily drawn into my little gambling games as we bet against the signal on the next set of traffic lights. We even had a bet riding on the way the chairman of the Amateur Snooker Board played with his glasses when he was making a speech. Mark reckoned he would always take them off in the middle of his address, so there we sat, watching for his hand. There was near miss after near miss. The hand would come up, touch the frame, only to go back down to the table. This went on and on as we tried like schoolkids to control our giggles. Tears were streaming down my face as he finished; the crowd of 400 bemused – Willie Thorne £10 richer.

I was proud to play for England and it had the added bonus of being exciting. The snooker halls and the crowds were getting bigger. I was playing with people I'd read about in magazines like *Snooker Scene*.

The real money in those amateur days was in league snooker. I was making a fair bit at Osborne's but there was more to be made playing for Standard Triumph at their social club in Coventry. Every Wednesday, I would travel across with Brian Cakebread, Rev Barry, Dave Barry, Gregg Baxter and Ally the Greek to Coventry, where the league standard was so much higher than in Leicester. There were over 20 players who had broken 100, whereas, in Leicester, there were only five. We soon picked up a crowd of 50 or more that would watch our four-frame matches, all of which were played for nothing. We were good. Rees would be capable of 60 or 70, while Brian was always likely to make a century break. With scoring potential like this, we were able to win the CIU, the biggest amateur tournament for three-men teams, three years on the trot.

Occasionally, we were challenged by teams like the really strong Welsh side of Doug Mountjoy, Des May and Alwyn Lloyd. A busload of us went down from Coventry with Rev Barry driving us. It was just like a jolly boys outing from *Only Fools and Horses*, with cratefuls of beer and lots of singing. There was a big contingent from Osborne's, a group that was to follow me everywhere, even when I turned professional and began touring abroad. We put a bet of £10,000 on ourselves and our fan club probably all had a couple of hundred pounds each. This was normal and it was becoming second nature to me.

The group from Osborne's was led by Racing Raymond Winterton; a huge, 25-stone guy, about ten years older than me. When I was making a reputation at Osborne's, we became friends. I was by now into horse racing, as it was a natural progression every day to drift from Osborne's into the bookmakers next door to chat about form and make a small bet. I was winning at snooker, so it was easy to fall into the habit of using all my winnings on my new passion.

Raymond had worked for his dad on the racetracks and, by now, he had inherited his pitches. He invited me down to a meeting and it was obvious to me that this was something I was going to love doing on regular basis. He soon taught me how to tick-tack and I became part of the team. It gave me the most incredible buzz every time we went to a course, though the thrill of Derby Day at Epsom was something really special. We used to have two pitches for that meeting, one in the Silver Ring and one on the hill at Tattenham Corner, so we would have a team of six away for a few days, having a laugh and staying in a nice hotel. It took very little to convince me that this was something special that I had drifted into. In the years that followed, we would do the same thing at Cheltenham, Goodwood and Royal Ascot – great weeks and warm memories.

Occasionally, I would clerk for Raymond, as I was good with figures, though that doesn't square up with my inability later on to manage my financial affairs. I used to love going with him to the tracks perhaps as much as twice a week, very often with a third or half stake in the book. I dealt with large sums of money every time we went racing and, in many ways, large amounts handled so regularly start to lose their value. They just become bundles of paper.

I loved the buzz of betting and laying odds and all that went with horse racing, especially those days when we won a lot of money. Sometimes we would win ten grand at a meeting, though we were just as likely to lose it the next time round. This went on every summer during the snooker closed season for five years. Eventually, as my face became known, I had to give up the tick-tack but my ties with the sport were so strong it had become part of my everyday life. By now, I had built up a knowledge of trainers, jockeys and horses' form. My betting stakes were building up too, but my new passion was under control and it just added to the thrill of being on a racecourse with thousands of other screaming punters.

The rest of the crew were all gamblers and snooker players at Osborne's. They were all mates who liked a drink and a bet. Years later, when I had climbed up the snooker ladder, they had a brief day of fame when the *Daily Mirror* wrote an article about the group of supporters who were following me round the big tournaments, like the World Championships. The leading lights of the group were 'Handbags' Barry (he sold handbags in the market), 'Billy the Dip' and the 'Red Faced Man' from Braunston. These people were not flash jack-the-lads. Red Face used to live at home and had to be in by midnight. His mother once phoned the police at 12.10am to report him missing after he had failed to show up. The biggest gambler was 'Have it on Vic'. He loved dog racing and would always put £50 on the favourite in the first race and then keep on doubling up to £100 in the second, £200 in the third and so on, in a pattern of relentless betting.

The group members were all genuine friends and were in no way hangers-on. We've had some great times together playing snooker, gambling, going on trips all over the country, having a laugh. You could say once again that Fate had intervened in my life. If I'd stayed at the Conservative Club, I would never have met them and perhaps I might have steered clear of gambling – but that's a very big 'perhaps'.

The Osborne years were great. I was a regular right up to the time I turned pro in 1975. I had my group of mates and it was flattering to be treated as the star of the club. By now, I'd added the National Under-19 title of 1973 to the one I'd won as Under-16 champion in 1970. I'd also won the national billiard championship four times (Under-16 in 1970, followed by Under-19 titles in 1971, 1972 and 1973). I grew from boyhood into manhood in that club and was treated like a son by the Osbornes and it was such a shame that, after all those years, the relationship suddenly ended after a huge row with Barry Osborne, the eldest son of the family. He'd returned to the club after being made redundant from his job and, looking back, he probably resented the way I treated the club as my office and training ground. I was used to picking up the phone in the club office, which was just to one side of the table area, whenever Mr and Mrs Osborne were scurrying around doing their jobs in the tearoom, or in the snooker room brushing down the tables, changing bulbs or one of the million other jobs they seemed to do.

One day, tensions came to a head when Barry found me on the phone arranging a challenge match. We had a terrible row as Barry harangued me about the way I treated the club as if I owned it. I was angry and hurt to realise that someone would think that of me. I loved the place and felt it was a huge part of my life. I asked for an apology but none ever came and so my ties with the club suddenly and unexpectedly came to an end. It was such a shame, because I'd learned so much, met so many great people and had so many good times there. But my biggest regret was that my relationship with Mr and Mrs Osborne was over. They were two lovely people, though not everybody's favourite couple. They had been so good to me in those early days of my snooker career and I will always be grateful to them for their kindness and support, but when the break came it was final. I never went back.

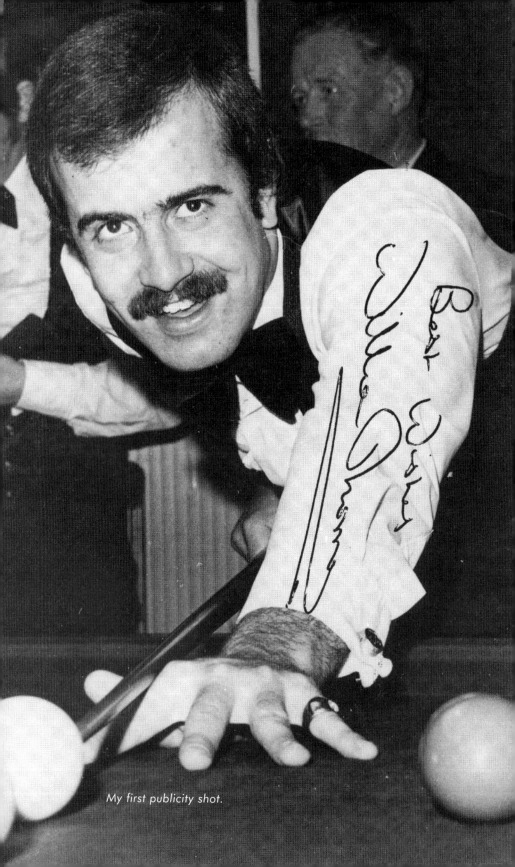

My first publicity shot.

chapter four
THE SNOOKER PRO

As an amateur international, I was coming into contact with a whole host of very talented players like Sid Hood, John Virgo, Joe Johnson and Tony Knowles. The latter two were my peers through the junior ranks, so I was never in awe of them. The player who did inspire me was John Spencer, who was one of the great World Champions. I remember travelling to Manchester with a group to see him play an exhibition match and he scored the first 147 I'd ever seen. There were probably 150 of us crammed into that working men's club and I can still recall the excitement. Lots of sports people can look back on their early years and remember a pivotal moment in their development. That 147 was so inspiring and it made me practise harder, with a fixation on getting that maximum break.

Soon after I became junior champion for the first time in 1970, I played Fred Davis at Evington Working Men's Club. Fred and Rex Williams were going round the country on the Watney Mann tour. The brewery had set up a travelling snooker stadium equipped with table, scoreboard and seating. They would play a nine-frame exhibition and then they would take on the local champ and another promising player. It was a big day for me and my parents as it was the first time I'd played in front of a really big audience. There were two or three hundred people watching, obviously drawn by two of the greatest snooker players of all time. I was getting a bit flash and played in a light brown suit, tie and shirt which my parents had bought me. I was only 16 and was carried along completely by the occasion. I was nervous but I beat him, even though I don't think I scored a break of more than 30 in the frame. I had a photo taken with Fred, who was really nice and very encouraging. When he told me how good I was for my age, my confidence was boosted up another rung – a wonderful, unforgettable and inspiring evening.

At this stage I was attracting my first bit of media attention. I'd get mentions in *Snooker Scene* and in the local press. My mum has still got my cuttings from the *Leicester Mercury* and she's probably got tapes of me being interviewed on *Midlands Today* and of the half hour programme *One on One* that I did for local radio.

By 1972, I had met a fair number of the big names in the game and, in that year, I came into contact with Alex Higgins for the first time. He was not a household name when he came to play in the Embassy World Championship, which was being held in Selly Park British Legion that year. My parents agreed to put him up during the Championship and, while he was staying with us, my mum used to iron his suit and shirt. He had brought all his gear down with him in a plastic supermarket bag – so Alex. He was with Simon Owen Sports Promotions at the time and an offer was made for me to be his chauffeur and right-hand man for the Championships. It was thought that being with him would help my game but I just didn't fancy it. I was only 18 and I wasn't ready for the job, especially as I was as a non-smoker and virtual teetotaller, hardly essential qualifications if I was to maximise the amount of time spent with him. I did manage a few practice games with Alex between sessions and later, I suppose, I felt a bit of a buzz when I realised that I'd just been playing with the man who was now World Champion.

By 1975, I was earning a reasonable living as an amateur snooker player. There didn't seem much point in following Fred Davis or John Spencer into the professional ranks, as I was earning a reasonable amount from challenge matches, betting on myself and from small tournament prizes. The circuit was still small and the boom which colour television was to bring to the game was still in its infancy. Then Ted Lowe came along and made me an offer I couldn't refuse.

Whispering Ted was synonymous with snooker for decades. He was the most wonderful man you could wish to meet. He was great for the game, lobbing little gems into the drama with his sotto voce contributions – "the hand of Tony Knowles", "the stance of Ray Reardon" (you have to read these in a Ted Lowe voice ...). He was 50 years in the game and yet he never called a shot correctly. He was a great lead commentator, leaving the colour commentary, as it's called in the trade, to the pro players, or to Clive Everton. Ted was also the author of one of the great 'Colemanballs' when commentating on a match between Fred Davis and Eddie Charlton. Fred was trying to reach over the table to play a shot when the cue ball was close to the cushion. He tried to reach it but realised he couldn't put his leg on the table, so he shaped to play the shot left handed but the cue ball was still out of reach. The timing was immaculate as everybody watched poor old Fred stretching and grimacing. Ted whispered unforgettably, "There you are, ladies and gentlemen. At sixty seven years of age, Fred Davis is a little bit too old to get his leg over." Not realising that the television audience was rolling around on the floor, Ted now dug himself an even deeper pit by adding, "I think Fred prefers to use his left hand instead."

Ted was, of course, the presenter of *Pot Black*, the show that had made such an impact on the game's popularity when it was launched in 1969. It was a half-hour programme in which just a single frame would be played. Tedious slow frames would be cleverly edited, while the short frames would be padded out with interviews, repeats of shots and analysis. It was a really successful formula, one that really took off with the spread of colour television and I jumped to accept Ted's invitation to play on the programme. I am so indebted to Ted for such an early opportunity, as I was to find out later that he had overridden the committee of the World Snooker Association to secure me the invitation.

I drove over to the Pebble Mill studios in Birmingham in December 1975. I was 21 and the holder of a whole boxful of business cards with the words, 'Willie Thorne: the World's Youngest Professional', emblazoned on them. Each card was silver with black writing and announced to the world that I was the UK junior champion, that my highest break was 141 and that I had scored over 300 centuries. It all seems a bit naff now but I was full of myself and couldn't wait to take on the challenge.

When I arrived, however, I actually felt rather overawed because I was playing with two of my heroes, John Spencer and Ray Reardon. There were five others recording with us over the next three days, producing a set of programmes that were to be shown over the summer of the following year on Wednesday evenings on BBC2. It was a round robin tournament played over that single short frame. We were told by the producers to try and finish in 20 minutes, which suited me and my style of play, as I've hardly played a frame that long in my life. Eddie Charlton could take 20 minutes a shot … Anyway, I managed to win a couple of games but I didn't make it to the semi-finals. I think I was only paid £500 but the effect of the exposure on my status in the game and my earning power was immediate and enormous. It seems unbelievable, nowadays, but to be *Pot Black* Champion was more important in those days than winning the Embassy World Championship. When Graham Miles won it he was able to play exhibitions for ten years afterwards as Pot Black Champion of 1974 and 1975.

I owe *Pot Black* more than just my first big break. It also gave me my first taste of big betting and a victory over the bookies. I had gone to Pebble Mill, two years before my debut, to watch the filming of *Pot Black* as a snooker fan. The transmission was a long time off and, at that time, there were no interviews and no articles in the press. Everybody, in fact, thought it was a live tournament.

I'd seen Graham's victory and thought nothing more of it until that summer, when I went down to the Isle of Wight to see my actress girlfriend who was appearing there in summer season. As I was passing a bookmaker's shop, I noticed a sign in the window giving the odds for *Pot Black*. Graham Miles was being offered at 20/1 for a tournament that I'd seen him win five months earlier! I had been gambling for some years by now but I'd never come across a dead cert like this before. It was like that fantasy when you can see into the future and you know exactly how things will turn out.

I kept this all to myself as I started to place bets in a pattern I was sure would not attract any attention. I would go into the shop to put a fiver on Ray Reardon, a couple of quid on Fred and then perhaps £20 on Miles. I used to go back and tell them that my Dad wanted ten quid on Reardon and £40 on Graham. I was able to repeat this a few times so, in the end, surprise, surprise, I cleared up well over a thousand pounds for absolutely nothing.

Appearing on *Pot Black* gave me the opportunity to do more exhibition work and I was able to charge a higher fee. I was trading on the fact that I was the youngest professional on the circuit. At 21, I was at least seven years the junior of everybody else. It had all come a bit too quickly I realise now, because there had been no careful

The photograph that was used on the cover of the Radio Times.

grooming process and I was soon made to feel like a fish out of water.

It didn't do me any harm, however, to appear shortly afterwards on the front cover of the *Radio Times* as the first snooker player ever to get such free, prominent publicity. The thinning hair and the thick black moustache were, I suppose, easily recognisable trademarks and I've been able to use and exploit them well into my career outside of snooker. I have had my moustache since I was 15 when the Beatles and others made is fashionable. It may be a bit old fashioned, but I'll never shave it off. It has been in a few places where it shouldn't have been and I wouldn't want to disturb the two Japanese soldiers who have been living in there since 1969.

I loved doing the exhibitions playing with people who were my peers. At first the fee was only £50 but it quickly increased to £250 as I received more exposure on television. I had a publicity photo made which went round all the snooker venues. It showed me cueing, with Graham Miles in the background signing autographs. This was all part of the process of building up a good living and pushing myself higher up the rankings.

Progress was difficult after I turned professional. I had probably made the step into the professional ranks too early and it was five years before I won my first tournament, the 1980 Pontin's Open. I was still only 26 and had a basic confidence in my own ability but I was inconsistent. Gambling was becoming an increasingly important part of my life as my income rose but, at this time, it was under control. I carried on going to the races, though not now as Racing Raymond's tick-tack man but as a real racing fan and enthusiastic punter. The buzz of being with lots of fellow gamblers is an almost indescribable feeling. Betting and winning are exciting in themselves but the general social crack of the courses makes the whole day at the races an intoxicating mix. I was a face by now and I was coming into contact with more and more wealthy people, lots of gamblers and wide boys. Unconsciously, I was building up a network of friends and contacts who recognised me as a gambler and, unfortunately, as it happened, someone the betting industry could give credit to as I pursued my gambling dreams.

I was still practising hard but my problem was my attitude when I was playing. Some days, I would be calm and self confident, whilst on other occasions, especially when I was playing some of the weaker players, I was nervous and my focus would drift. My concentration was fine when I was playing against the top players but I would throw matches away when playing someone like Murdo McLeod. I once lost to him 5-4 after making a 90 break and three centuries. In other games, I couldn't make a 20. This was a function of the nine-frame match format, when every frame is important and form upsets are more likely. Doubts were soon sown in your mind when you lost a frame and you started to think that another four like that and you would be out. In longer matches, in tournaments like the World Championships and the UK Championships, I did reasonably well, with the pressure to win each frame being far lower. You could lose a frame or two through bad luck, or a single poor shot, but you would be far less anxious about making up lost ground.

I never lost my self belief in those early years. In practice and in matches I was always capable of scoring centuries and even a 147. My attitude, however, was often negative and, in those days, there were no psychological coaches to help me produce a more positive approach to the game. I really needed help when I was in a winning position. I was always thinking in a frame about what would happen to me if I got into a winning position. Would I lose like last time? If I missed a couple of shots, the doubts would set in and I'd be saying to myself, "Here it goes again".

My temperament cost me, especially when playing at the World Championships. I lost a match I should have won against Bill Werbenuik in the last 16 and it was to have long, lingering effects. The following year, I was 12-9 up against Eddie Charlton with an easy black to win. My mind went back to the previous year and the tension got the better of me. I missed it. I was still 12-10 in the lead but my game fell to pieces as Eddie started to play well. I didn't win another frame and he won the last three frames easily.

Besides this fundamental lack of big match temperament, I wasn't particularly driven at this stage of my career. I was basically happy with my lot as a fairly well paid snooker pro, winning through the early rounds of most of the tournaments I entered. Yet despite all of my weaknesses, I still felt that I had the ability to become World Champion one day. I knew deep down that I wasn't in the same class as Reardon but, even accounting for all his flair and ability, I was not worried about Higgins, the other top player at the time. But Alex, like Dennis Taylor in his prime, could be a different class as a match player. They were both match hard with fantastic temperaments. I was probably 21 points better as a break-builder than Dennis but the game of snooker is not just about potting balls; it is about attitude and keeping your composure and avoiding the plague of twitching. When I put myself under pressure, my cueing hand would move the cue sideways as I brought it back before hitting the cue ball. You tighten up and what was your well practised cue action is just not there anymore and you find yourself potting balls from memory. Some people have drawn the comparison with the yips in golf when players lose control over the club in the vital area of putting. Both ailments are psychological but twitching's nearest equivalents are in hooking and slicing on the golf course, when you inexplicably move away from the normal plane of your swing.

Snooker, of all games, must be the most difficult one in which to keep your concentration. There are so many minutes of each frame when you are sitting in your chair watching your opponent play, willing him to miss a shot but also watching the way the pack is set up to plan your next opening. Fortunately for me, I was a quick player. I could make a 100 break in six minutes, so keeping my focus over such a short period was easy. At this level of concentration, I was very good but, if I had to endure a spell of lengthy breaks by my opponent, my mind would wander and my concentration would evaporate.

Outside pressures also took their toll throughout my career. My gambling, especially when I was going through a losing streak, caused my attention to stray, although, occasionally, something happened that was beyond my control.

In 1982, in the year he became World Champion, I faced Alex Higgins in the quarter final at the Crucible. I had been playing well and had breezed through the early rounds. Although I had never made it to the last eight before, I was feeling fairly confident about my own game and I was hoping that Alex would have one of his off-days. However, on the morning of the match my face was plastered all over the front page of the *Sun*. The story claimed that I'd been having an affair and the cuckolded husband had gone missing and, according to the article, had taken his shotgun with him. Apparently, he had shot a hole through the wall of their house when he accused his wife of watching a video of me playing rather than taping *Not the Nine O'Clock News*. She liked to have a laugh.

My brother drove me up from Leicester that morning. I was scared to death and my concentration was in tatters. Alex Higgins was the last person on my mind – I had another nutter to occupy my thoughts. When the match started, I felt really paranoid; it seemed as if everyone in the theatre was watching my every move. I started the match well and notched up a break of 143 in the morning. The pressure was still there and Higgins did not help the situation, or my tangled nerves, by having a go at me in an interview with the Press. His little throwaway line, "Willie Thorne would stab his own mother for fifty pence", hurt me as I thought he had more respect for my family and for me.

My game deteriorated and I was eliminated. I was seething with anger about the timing of the story's release. I had hoped that, at last, this was to be my big year and my real breakthrough into the top rank of snooker. Everything had happened a week before but the *Sun* chose the morning of this crucial match to reveal it to the nation. As it happened, it was a non-story. The fugitive husband was arrested after his car had been traced and dramatically surrounded by a police squad. The gun was found in the boot but the explanation that it had been put there for a hunting trip was accepted. He claimed he was not after me at all and the whole incident had been a series of misunderstandings. The damage had been done; I was out at the quarter final stage of the World Championships.

Snooker's appeal was now growing beyond our shorelines and I had a ranking high enough to be invited to play in tournaments abroad to help popularise the game. My first trip abroad was to play on the burgeoning snooker circuit in Canada. I was taken over with John Virgo by Maurice Hayes, the first real snooker entrepreneur and promoter to take the financial risk of opening up this new market in North America. Snooker was dwarfed by the game of pool over there and was still in its infancy. There was limited television coverage in the early 1980s, though Canada was building up a group of talented local players. Three of them, Cliff Thorburn, Kirk Stevens and Bill Werbenuik had very successful careers in Britain but there were others who tried their luck over here and only had some short term success. Jim Wych, Brady Golan and Bob Paquet had their moments but nothing like Bob Chaperon, who managed to win the British Open title. This was one of the biggest fluke results of all time. Racing Raymond had been on holiday at the time, so when asked for the odds he would have given against Chaperon winning it he said, "A hundred to one, no more. Why are you asking?" I told him the result and there was just this long silence before he spluttered and laughed down the phone, "You're having me on ... who won it really?"

I enjoyed going over to Canada, so much so, in fact, that I competed for ten seasons on the trot in the C and E Tournament held in Toronto. We had some great laughs and I just loved the life of playing exhibitions and, of course, gambling, in such a pleasant part of the world. John Virgo had been a friend since junior tournament days and was now my playing partner and my companion in so many escapades away from the snooker hall. I remember that we stayed in a log cabin out of town on a first trip. Perhaps we had other things on our minds in those days, as I remember being locked out of our place one freezing cold afternoon and then spending four bone-chilling hours sitting on a chair swing, chatting and putting the world to rights. John wandered off as the cold got to him and the next thing I sensed was the light suddenly going on in the kitchen. We'd forgotten to lock the back door! The air had been so cold that afternoon it had left us several centimetres shorter but we were like a couple of filleted men, doubled up, crying, collapsed in laughter.

The Canadian snooker scene never really grew beyond those promising beginnings. Just when things were about to take off as Thorburn ground his way to the Embassy World Championship, there were revelations about Cliff and Bill in the tabloid press. Thorburn's marijuana habit and Werbenuik's gargantuan drinking sprees were splashed across the papers and the coverage was

The perfect number plate for Maximum Man.

Celebrating my win at Pontin's with Mum.

sufficient for the vital television deals to start to dry up in Canada.

India was a major contrast to Canada in so many ways. The game had far deeper roots in the sub-continent, partly because snooker had actually been invented there by a group of British Army Officers in the late nineteenth century and partly because the other table game of billiards had been popular, with its roots in India going back many hundreds of years. Snooker had grown in popularity by the time of the boom in Britain and, by the 1980s, had a certain social cachet amongst the Indian middle classes. We used to have exhibitions at sumptuous places like the Bombay Gymkhana on our way to Australia. Our games were played in front of large, appreciative, well-to-do audiences and yet, less than a 100 yards away from the hotel, there was the most pitiable poverty imaginable.

When we first arrived, we stopped briefly in a queue of traffic on our way from the airport to the hotel and immediately the hand of a crippled child came through the taxi window. I felt shocked and so ignorant. I realised that I had lived in ignorance, unaware of this other world, never watching the news, or keeping up with current affairs. I felt a deep sense of guilt. I could not bear the poverty and my knee-jerk reaction was to give away money to beggars and any other unfortunate every time we were approached on those trips outside the hotel. As time has gone on and throughout all my self-imposed difficulties, experiences like those in India have made me want to give my money and time generously for charities. It's easy to forget how others live their lives when you are carried along as a highly paid sportsman living a self indulgent life style with its hotel living, cars, houses and expensive foreign holidays. Sermon over …

Australia was on our itinerary at least once a year. Snooker had maintained a high profile in that country, largely because of a sporting icon, Eddie Charlton. He was a national hero and someone so revered that he was chosen to carry the Olympic torch. Moreover, he was an excellent player and someone who was very underrated.

The game in Australia was very television driven in the 1980s. Snooker shows were transported all over the vast distances of the continent in a juggernaut. A small snooker 'stadium' with seating and the match table would be unfolded for the televised matches as it travelled from state to state.

Eddie Charlton's presence beside the British professionals was essential for the growth of the game. Many British fans tended to dismiss him as just a boring, slow player, but he wasn't: he was fantastic. Admittedly, he used to take a long time over each shot. He used to clean the black, white and pink before every frame. Every chalk mark was removed from the table as part of the meticulous routine followed at every match. This was Eddie's nature. His car was always checked each time he used it for tyre pressure, oil and water. His suitcase was always packed neatly in sections with items taken out nightly, rerolled and then replaced. When he was playing in a tournament, he always brought a little bag with him containing a cloth, mirror and comb. He would disappear to the gents for ten minutes and reappear looking immaculate. A great character and a great player.

South Africa was another regular point of call and a place I'll always associate with David Taylor, the Silver Fox. We roomed together from time to time and I very quickly found that he was a hypochondriac. He was a walking pharmacy with pills and ointments for every ailment under the sun. Soon after we'd arrived on one trip, I started to feel really bloated as the effects of constipation started to kick in. David, of course, had the antidote, a laxative pill that would solve my problem. I took two tablets instead of the single recommended dose but nothing happened. That night we went out for an Indian and, sure enough, halfway through the main course things started to happen. My chair shot back as I rushed out for the first of 20 visits to the throne! Back in the hotel an hour later, I got out the mirrors to check on the state of the exit hatch. It felt as if there had been a fire blazing away between my buttocks and I was starting to panic. Sure enough, my worst fears were well founded; the mirrors showed a huge swelling like an over-ripe, tropical fruit. I began writing my application form to be guest primate in the baboon sector of the nearest game reserve, the Kruger National Park. I shouted at Taylor, "Look what your pills have done to my arse." Without blinking, David replied, "I've got the very cream ..."

We actually visited the Kruger some days later and stayed in a hotel lodge. We were told there were thousands of elephants in the area of the park where we were staying but after our fourth day we'd seen nothing. We were getting a bit desperate for souvenirs and even a decent photograph or two by this stage, so we picked up a huge snail we saw being attacked by a bird. We scared the bird away and took the snail, which was about the size of my fist, back to the hotel. We left it on the bed and then went to the bar for a sundowner. We told our story to the bar room philosophers gathered there and, naturally, there is always one with doom and gloom advice. "You'd better go and find it. Those snails always look for somewhere warm at night. They could be in your bed, under your arm, up your jacksee and … they're poisonous."

We belted back to the room and started to turn it upside down, throwing sheets and blankets everywhere, ripping out drawers in a frantic search for the deadly crustacean. This went on for ages until there was a knock at the door. We were pouring with sweat by now. It was the maid. "Oh yes", she said, "I saw the snail on the bed and thought I'd better get rid of it and so I threw it out the window." Tears came into my eyes as I looked around the devastated room …

As snooker boomed in the mid-80s, we were also invited to the Gulf, to places like Dubai. By now I was with Barry Hearn's Matchroom organisation and we were commanding high fees and staying in fantastic hotels. There was a large ex-pat following for the game out there and, in the days before the explosion of satellite television, there was a large audience for live snooker. Prize money helped, of course, in attracting the best the game could offer.

New Zealand was added to the circuit and we set off with Ian Doyle's Cuemasters, flying club class from Heathrow. Dennis and I had probably been given the invite because we'd built up a reputation by this stage for our ability to talk to sponsors and do the corporate hospitality bit. We were good at mingling and bullshitting – a talent that has never left me.

When the players arrived at Heathrow, we were all suited up, unlike Stephen Hendry, Ian Doyle's new protégé. I had a contact at the airport – Francis de Souza, who worked in corporate hospitality and public relations at Terminal 4. Dennis Taylor and I went to see him and managed to get him to wangle an upgrade to First Class. We were regular customers and Francis was such a useful contact as he could always get us these upgrades. As we were moving down the runway the stewardess allowed me to use the PA system. "Mr Thorne and Mr Taylor request the company of other members of Cuemasters in the first class lounge for drinks after take-off. No jeans or cowboy boots admitted."

When we arrived, I managed to win the tournament and was feeling pretty good about myself as it was a high profile event, playing in the New Zealand parliament building in front of the Prime Minister and a smattering of celebrities, including Simply Red, who were on tour at the time. As I was the tournament winner, I was probably the prime target for a wind-up that everybody loved playing. I suspected nothing when I got a phone call inviting me to be a judge at the Miss New Zealand beauty contest. I accepted and managed to get an invite for Dennis Taylor as well but, rather curiously, he told me he wasn't up to it after a hard week of snooker.

I was told by the organisers that a limousine would be round at the hotel at 5.30 to take me to the contest. I waited in the hotel foyer, dress suited, looking anxiously at my watch as the minutes ticked by, 6.40 no limousine … 6.50 still no sign of the vehicle. Then there was a phone call to tell me that my transport was stuck in traffic and that I would have to take a cab. The cab came and I realised that all I could tell the cabbie was to take me to the Miss New Zealand contest. He seemed bemused but he tried three or four possible venues before he brought me back to the hotel. I was panicking and starting to seethe with anger – I hate being late. Another cabbie then came into the foyer and told me that he'd been given instructions to take me to the Miss New Zealand contest. I still suspected nothing as he dropped me off to be greeted by Dennis Taylor. Dennis led me through a set of double doors, where a guard of honour of the Cuemasters was waiting to applaud me into a … Chinese restaurant. Everybody had been in on it, Dennis, the driver, the receptionist and, I suspect, Stephen Hendry. Revenge was sweet.

Celebrating winning the Mercantile Classic with Phil Neal, Bruce Grobbelaar and Gary.

chapter five
BREAKTHROUGH

It wasn't easy working my way up the professional ranks. I was earning a good living but it took me seven years to win my first major tournament at Pontin's in 1982. I had made the World Champions Quarter finals that year, as well, but I still wasn't winning the really big tournaments. That win at the Pontin's camp in Prestatyn meant that for the 1982-83 season I was in the top 16 at last. The following year, I built on this success by reaching the semi-final of the Grand Prix – the first time I'd made it to the ranking stage of a tournament.

My breakthrough was to come in 1985 when I won my biggest prize of £40,000 as I defeated Cliff Thorburn in the final of the Mercantile Credit Classic at Warrington. My close pal, Gary Lineker, was in the crowd. There was a massive television audience, in excess of 12 million, but it is always good to play in front of a live audience who you know are going to give you support, and Warrington was a prime example of this. I had my racing crowd from the Osborne days, plus my family and a spattering of sporting celebrities I'd met, such as Bruce Grobbelaar, Phil Neal and Tony Sibson, the Leicester champion boxer. I have always attracted that sort of fan, famous in their own right, and it has always done my ego a lot of good when somebody in the public eye has complimented me. Jim Bowen was the compère of the cult quiz show, *Bullseye* in the mid-80s. I'd never met him but, on the morning of the final, I got a phone call from him, completely out of the blue, to tell me that he was a big fan and he was hoping I'd win the big one after all these years of trying. As a player with a very fragile mental approach to the game, it was a real boost to my confidence for him take the trouble to find me before one of the biggest matches of my life.

I had been a nearly man for a long time but I was not prepared for the strange emotion that hit me after that victory. There was a huge television audience, wild applause, interviews and back slapping but all I could think about was the sense of anti-climax that surrounded me.

Nineteen eighty-six was another good year for me as I reached the quarter finals of the Crucible again and made the finals of two major tournaments, the UK and the British Open. I maintain to this day that I should have won the UK at Preston. I was 13-8 up against Steve Davis in the 31-frame final going into the last session. Gary Lineker had come to the hotel to see me before the session to give me his support and his little pep talk. I know he didn't mean to give me the jitters, but when you're lacking in mental strength as I was, one phrase, no matter how innocently meant, can lodge itself in your head. "One more frame and he'd need to beat you eight one to win the match."

"I know, I know. There's no way I can lose the way I'm playing."

I went out to play, feeling fairly confident, though trying to get that phrase of Gary's out of my head … "One more frame … One more frame … One more frame …"

I was 40 behind in the first frame but then everything started to flow in my direction as I got on to the final four reds. A big winning break seemed to be there for the taking. I started clearing up. I moved on to the colours and went quickly through the yellow, green and brown. I was on the blue now. No problem at all. I can't miss. I can't be beaten. I hit the blue almost without thinking. The delivery felt fine. There was no hint of twitching and I didn't get a bad contact. I was trying to roll the cue ball through to the pink so I stunned it to save me a walk around the table. Oh no … the blue was jawed!

I went back to my seat and the doubts kicked in straightaway. Gary's phrase came back almost like a mantra I couldn't shake out of my head. I was still 13-9 in front but all I could think about was the way I'd failed in big games in the past. This was the demon I had to wrestle with for the next two or three years, when I should really have been winning more tournaments. I was in my prime. I reached the final of the Irish Masters in both 1986 and 87 but lost both, although I did manage to win a couple of minor tournaments, the Hong Kong Masters and the Matchroom Tournament.

Celebrating with, from the left, Relentless Reg, Billy the Dip, Racing Raymond, myself, Captain John, Gary, Tony Sibson and friend.

A proud moment shared with Dad.

I was confident of my own ability but whenever I got into a winning position, I just felt my opponents were thinking, "I've still got a chance against Willie". Friends have often said that other players would play well against me because they knew I was fallible and that I had a dodgy track record in crossing that winning line. Basically, people weren't frightened of me and that made it so much harder to win.

The Davis match was so important and a pivotal one in my career. Admittedly, I was near the top of my chosen profession and I was earning lots of money. I had all the trappings of fame; a big house in Great Glen on the edge of Leicester, expensive cars and foreign holidays. The basic point for me was that I could never see that missed blue in terms of money. I had backed myself heavily to win a lot of money but it was about winning a snooker final, about beating Steve Davis, the best player in the world and getting the same kick as I did when I beat Ray Reardon, six times champion, in the UK Open.

These peak years in my career coincided with the great boom in snooker. Barry Hearn and his organisation were responsible in many ways for popularising the game and earning me lots of money. He had invited me to join his Matchroom team in 1985 and I was to stay with him until 1992. There was no way I could begrudge the 20 per cent of my snooker income that went to Barry as he was getting me invitations to tournaments under the umbrella of Matchroom. Without this connection, I would have missed out on so many of the minor (but lucrative) tournaments and exhibitions. Barry had organised that Matchroom tournament amongst his players and was able to attract lots of sponsorship money plus the television rights so that the first prize was £50,000, which I was able to win.

In the final, I played Steve Davis and was losing 9-8. In the corner of my eye I could see Barry poised with a bottle of champagne. The event was being shown on Sky and that sort of reception would have been in keeping with the image that Barry was trying to create for Steve. The effect was dramatic and I cleared the table and went on to make a break of 80 in the final frame to win the match. I don't know what happened to the bottle of champers but it didn't matter, as all my nutcases had come down from Leicester and we had our own special party.

Barry was always looking for ways to make money out of the snooker boom and out of Matchroom. Out came the Matchroom after-shave from the deal he'd made with Goya, the slippers, the chalk, the cue cases – all of them designed to ride the wave that everybody in snooker was on. The foray into the field of pop music was inevitable in those days. The 70s and 80s, decades notorious for naff sports records, had given us toe-squirmers like the horrendous *Back Home* sung by the England football team before the 1970 World Cup finals. Our contribution to this piece of culture was a cut above this. Steve Davis, Tony Meo, Jimmy White, Dennis Taylor and Terry Griffiths were roped in by Barry to make the unforgettable *Snooker Loopy*. It was written for us by Chas and Dave, recorded over three days and then released to the ears of the British public. Who could resist verses like the one dedicated to me?

Old Willie Thorne
His hair's all gone
His mates all take the rise
His opponents said
Cover up your head
Cos it's shining in my eyes
When the lights shine down
To say he's going to walk it
It's not fair
Giving off that glare
Perhaps we'll have to chalk it

Well I liked it and so did 45,000 other people who bought it and made it number five in the charts. If only the *Chicken Song* had not been the nation's favourite at the time ... but there's another of my excuses. We did a follow up, *The Romford Rap*, but mysteriously it only made it to number 45, even though it was a better record, honest ...

The album deal, 147 Snooker Songs, didn't materialise, to the regret of the whole nation, but we'd had such a great time recording, making a video and television appearances, that it didn't matter. It was a time we all look back on with great fondness because we had become so famous, so recognisable and so marketable. We were living the lifestyle of celebrities, making appearances at theatres, regattas and race meetings and revelling in the attention we were getting. Andy Warhol's ration of 15 seconds of fame was exceeded and, if you ask anybody who has been famous even for a short time, it is an intoxicating feeling and one that is often difficult for some people to give up.

After 1988, I slipped out of the top eight but I was still earning a lot from snooker. The new endorsements in the game were going to the new breed of players like Stephen Hendry, but I was still capable of earning the occasional big sum from getting the highest break in the tournament and through exhibitions. Barry Hearn was, by now, devoting more of his entrepreneurial energy to boxing where he was managing Chris Eubank. Just as he discovered Steve Davis, he was now looking after another World Champion. Later, of course, he took over Prince Nazeem's affairs and then diversified into a whole host of other ventures – Pool TV, Leyton Orient football club, ten-pin bowling and fishing as a television sport. We parted in 1992. It was an amicable divorce. I owe a lot to Barry, who was a clever, decent bloke and someone with immense enthusiasm for everything he has tried. I would never slag him off to anyone within or outside the game.

Snooker changed so much in the 1980s and the influence of the Matchroom organisation was important in setting standards. The image of snooker changed markedly during that decade, as it moved away from the spit and sawdust days of the snooker and billiard halls. There were still some connections to those old traditional days. At one time players used to drink when they were playing. As the game became an increasingly popular television sport, the PBSA, anxious to establish a more squeaky clean image, banned drinking alcohol after a period when players drank quite openly in front of the cameras. Others, like Rex Williams, had a shot of whisky to calm their nerves before they went out to play. The Canadians, Stevens, Thorburn and Werbenuik all drank, Bill downing as many as ten pints of lager a day to calm his nerves (allegedly). Alex Higgins would often be seen sipping gin and tonic in the players' seating area as his opponent was playing.

Despite all the temptations, I have never been a drinker. Nowadays, I will drink the occasional glass of wine or a can of Red

Bull to help me concentrate on a long drive. Mickey Gunn, the comic, warned me recently about the high level of female hormones in the drink. Apparently, if you have six or more Red Bulls you get a headache, lose the ability to drive and get an uncontrollable urge to go shopping …

The organisers were in more of a dilemma over the issue of smoking. The World Championships have long been associated with Embassy cigarettes as the major sponsor, while Benson and Hedges have also sponsored a major tournament. Alex Higgins was going to be a major problem, as he was an inveterate smoker, sometimes having two cigarettes on the go at the same time. He'd leave them in the players' seated area while he was at the table. Whenever I played him, I used to take a great delight in stubbing them out, partly through distaste as I have never been a smoker, and partly as a psychological gambit. I am sure it had little or no effect, because Alex was such a hard match player, always focused. Still, it made me feel good for a few seconds. When he finished a break, he would always be back, lighting up almost before he sat down. The compromise deal, nowadays, has been to ban cigarettes in the auditorium, while allowing the players to carry on smoking. The BBC have a policy of moving the cameras away whenever a player looks as if he is about to smoke.

Snooker has had a good image for many years. There is hardly any backbiting in the game, with the present Mark Williams / Ronnie O'Sullivan spat a marked exception. The tabloid press, of course, are only too willing to dig up dirt on players and exaggerate arguments. I rarely had a problem with other players. The only person I ever fell out with was Higgins. We had a great time together on numerous occasions but Alex is simply so unpredictable. We'd just finished playing in a snooker exhibition in Canada, close to a huge fairground where everybody seemed to be winning huge teddy bears. I suddenly realised that I had not bought anything for my girlfriend back in England and we were flying back the next day. Try as I could that night I just could not win one, so out of desperation, I bought the bear Alex Higgins had won.

On the plane going back, Higgins, predictably, got drunk and tried to grab the teddy from me. A fight broke out and I managed

A typical snooker gathering with Rex Williams on my right and Alex
Higgins, Jimmy White and the late John Pulman on my left.

Racing Raymond and myself flank Ray Reardon, who is holding the
Yamaha Organ International Masters Trophy.

to give him a smack before the others pulled us apart. This was our version of the Five Mile High Club, although not as pleasurable. There is a whole litany of people who have hit Alex during his long career. He once wound up Cliff Thorburn to such an extent that, even after they'd been separated, the Grinder was so mad he immediately smacked him in the face.

Alex is a genuine eccentric and has done many strange and whacky things. On one of our trips I remember being in the next room to him in a hotel when suddenly I heard him knocking on the wall, shouting for me to come through.

"What do you want?" I demanded.

"I want to show you something," he screamed back at me.

I got up and, like I had done so many times before, I started to try to predict the unpredictable. I went in to discover him there on the bed, stone cold sober, lying back and displaying his freshly shaven bollocks. "What do you think of this, Willie?"

I paused. "I think it might be the way forward ...," I replied, trying to imagine a reply from the Queen Mother if found in the same situation.

Pot Black had given snooker such a great start in the 70s but it was the televising of the World Championships when it was moved to Sheffield that gave the game its biggest boost. After the Higgins final of 1972, television coverage gradually increased, though it was still overshadowed by the one-frame version of the game that television had popularised. By 1974, it was still in its infancy but the final between Graham Miles and Ray Reardon was at last shown live from Wythenshawe. The tournament that year had been divided into a northern and southern section, with one semi-final being played in Middlesbrough and the other in the Manchester suburb of Wythenshawe.

Ray was a great player who had already been champion twice and was obviously determined to repeat his success of the previous year when he had defeated Eddie Charlton by the mammoth score of 38-22. Matches this long were far too unwieldy for television and so the 1974 final was played over 43 frames, hardly a giant forward step and a format which could only be shown in highlight form. Ray was to win easily, 22-12 but not until he had made protests about the table. Graham had won the southern section (Mancunians must have been staggered by this description) and Ray complained that this gave Miles an advantage. I'd hardly put this in the category of gamesmanship, but Ray was obviously keen to reduce any psychological advantage he thought this gave Graham. So the table was changed.

By the time the Championships went live on television in 1977, the venue had been moved to what is now virtually the game's spiritual home, the Crucible Theatre in Sheffield. The final was still a very long, best of 49 frames format, which was far too unwieldy for live television. Only four days were allocated to televising the tournament and so the coverage had to be limited to the semi-final and final stages. Ray Reardon won his sixth Embassy World Championship, defeating the South African, Perrie Mans 25-18 in the final but, perhaps, the more significant statistic was the viewing audience of 7 million. The feedback from the viewing public was so good that the BBC decided to show all 13 days of the tournament on BBC2 the following year. Snooker had really arrived.

The Crucible is a theatre in the round and so it is a great venue for snooker. It has become the snooker equivalent of Wembley or Wimbledon and I still get an enormous buzz even when I drive past the place. It is actually part of a three theatre complex called the Sheffield Theatres. The Crucible is the largest of the theatres but its capacity is only 960 which means that it is just not big enough. The Lyceum section is left as a theatre during the 17 day event but the Studio acts as a two table practice area and the television set for the BBC commentary team. The backstage area is awful. So much is cheap and makeshift but, I suppose, all of that is inevitable given the fact that the complex caters for snooker for just a short period every year. The stairways are just temporary hardboard affairs and the famous curtains that players step through as they are introduced to the crowd are made of flimsy cheap cloth.

The Crucible has a sunken stage and the floor you see on television is actually supported by a system of jacks which hold the two one and a half ton tables, plus the players, who included the 20-stone Bill Werbenuik at one stage. When you are playing, you are acutely aware of the closeness of the crowd and the sound-proof boxes that are constructed for the commentary team, the Press and photographers. The camera technology has changed radically over the years and is less obtrusive than in the 70s and 80s. At least eight cameras are in use for each game, nowadays, with pocket cameras a recent addition but the basic fault of the arena is the limited amount of floor space – making it difficult for the cameras to move around. In my early days, there were just four large television cameras which would move within a foot of the pocket and could be hugely distracting. It took me at least a couple of tournaments to get used to them but, to be honest, when your concentration is really good and highly focused, you don't notice the cameras. It was the same when you were playing with the screen dividing you from the game next door. If your concentration was poor, you would hear every clap, cough and fart coming from the other game's audience.

The tournament attracts its fair share of snooker anoraks from all over the world. There is one guy from the States who has his annual holiday in Sheffield. He is a big bloke who makes a real occasion out of it, always in a suit and never missing a session. You see people like this year after year and, I suppose, it is inevitable that we lose the occasional regular. One of Tony Drago's fans, a ten-year regular, died in his chair and nobody sat there for the rest of the tournament as a mark of respect.

The crowd is very knowledgeable but it has definite favourites. In the early rounds, there are often a lot of empty seats when the lesser known players are appearing but they always bring their supporters and their cheering always creates an atmosphere even in a sparsely populated hall.

It is always an advantage to have supporters in the crowd as they undoubtedly lift you. Gary Lineker was always very inspiring. He was always to be relied on for giving little tips, especially about my levels of concentration. He always found his way to the Crucible and usually managed to get a seat, or worm his way on to the gantry.

Whenever White or Higgins played, it was a very different story. I never really enjoyed the experience as I felt almost like the bad guy. There would be a cheer if I missed an easy shot, though to be fair their supporters are fairly restrained when you compare them with the audiences I have played in front of in Thailand. I remember a match against James Wattana in front of a very partisan crowd of about 400 in a hotel in Bangkok. There were probably another 1,000 people watching the match on closed-circuit TV all over the building. In the game, I remember screwing into the pack and, three kisses later, watching the cue ball disappearing into the pocket. Then I was deafened by the cheering from all over the hotel as I realised I had lost the match 5-4 and that I was the only guy for miles around who wasn't celebrating. It was not the greatest of feelings.

Steve Davis was the most focused player I have ever watched or played against. He claims that he did not have any special technique to enable him to concentrate. He has always kept himself physically fit throughout his playing career and I am sure that it has helped his game, just as it has added to the games of Hendry, John Higgins and Mark Williams. I went through a spell towards the end of my career when I employed a personal trainer. She had been an Olympic athlete and she recommended a regime of stretching exercises. I could see the logic in exercising and I did feel the short-term benefit of all the exercises I was put through but, by that stage, I had lost the hunger and my hand-eye coordination was not what it had been.

Within two months, I had given up that fad and I moved on to the next one. I went on diets towards the end of my career, mainly to keep my weight down, but also to improve my general fitness and well-being. I went through so many crazes at this stage of my career, just to try to keep my sharpness, as the competition from younger players grew more and more intense. I could not sleep before the big games and so I was often knackered in really long matches. My mind would often wander to the bets I had on for the next day and the recurring thought that I had just not given my career 100 per cent throughout my time in the game.

Davis was probably the first player to employ a coach and to use positive mental attitude techniques and what is now known as sports psychology. Whenever I played him, I noticed the way in which he would pick out a spot somewhere around the table. He would fix his glare on a flower in one of the arrangements, or a spot on the carpet, and then use it to shut out all distractions.

On other occasions, I saw him rummage in his waistcoat pocket and take out a piece of paper. I don't know what it said. Maybe it was just a dry cleaning bill or a little tip – 'Keep your head still', or perhaps it just said, 'Willie is useless. You've got nothing to beat'. No matter what the secret of his success was, he dominated snooker throughout the 80s, winning the World Championships six times. Steve is the game's greatest ambassador, a truly marvellous player.

John Higgins and Mark Williams are the two modern players who spring to mind if we are looking for the successors to 'Interesting' Steve. They both have the ability to shut out the memory of bad shots. I could never do that. I would brood, never able to push them to the back of my mind.

Behind the bar at my Snooker Centre.

chapter six
MY SNOOKER CENTRE

During the boom years of snooker, Leicester, my home city, was to enjoy a close association with the game. Until 1980, there was just a handful of traditional billiard halls, spit and sawdust establishments like the Osborne's. There was only one proper snooker centre in England at the time and that was the one in Leeds run by Jim Williamson. He opened in 1978 on Kirkstall Road and made such a success of it that we decided, as the Thorne family, to open the Willie Thorne Snooker Centre.

My mother and brothers were my partners in the venture as my father and mother had gone their separate ways. He was still running the Shoulder of Mutton but had now renamed it the Falcon. He was earning enough money from the licensed trade to indulge his new habit of gambling. He also owned a racehorse which he was to call, rather insensitively, Lana's Secret. I use the term 'insensitively' because Lana was the name of the daughter of the woman who'd succeeded my mother as his partner at the pub. My parents' marriage had not been a happy one and my childhood had not been without its upsets, as my Dad was often rough with my mother, as well as with my brothers and me. There were lots of arguments and rows and, I suppose, it was no surprise when she walked out of the pub. She has never said it, but I really think she only stayed with him for the sake of her three boys. She had reached the stage where she had had enough, and my father's new relationship was the last straw. She packed up and moved to a little terraced house in Tudor Road, near the centre of Leicester.

My brothers, Robert and Malcolm, were also part of the snooker centre scheme. We had little money between us but everybody was so confident that we were going to be successful that they both packed in their jobs, Malcolm in the shoe trade with Stead and Simpson and my younger brother, Robert, who was then an apprentice butcher. The Snooker Centre was created as a property conversion on Charles Street, with Jim Williamson's club as our

Dad with his horse, Lana's Secret.

template. As we only had £15,000 initially to invest, we had to duck and dive cleverly. Obviously, as a starting point we needed an architect to draw up our plans and we were lucky enough to negotiate an arrangement for the monthly payments of his fees. I managed to secure a large loan from the bank after convincing them that the centre was going to be a goldmine. It helped, of course, to be able to trade on my name, as I was appearing on television and was becoming quite well known.

The club design which the architect came up with was almost like a hotel. There was a bar area as well as a restaurant serving as many as 50 meals at lunchtimes. It was carpeted throughout and the wood panelling everywhere gave it quite a classy, opulent feel. The tables were the most important items in making the place a success. Nowadays, a full-sized table will cost in excess of £7,000 and so our outlay on the essential equipment was to cut deep into our bank loan. Fortunately, we were able to buy our tables from Jack Karnham. He must have realised that we were opening a potential gold mine and would be major customers for a long time, as he told us we could pay him back as soon as we had the money.

Our optimism was proved right. In those days, you could basically open up a barn, put tables in it and, before you knew it, you would be making four grand a week through snooker and one armed bandits. We made a lot of money from the Snooker Centre before my debts started to build up. It was also a place that I used both as an essential practice area now that my connection with Osborne's had gone and as a social centre. A lot of the good local players were attracted to the club and so playing standards were high. Players used to use the bar and all the other spin-offs you get whenever you join a club. We used to arrange regular go-karting nights near Newark, down the A46 from Leicester. Gary Lineker was a young soccer pro in those days but he distanced himself from this side of the club, telling us all that there was no way he'd go and risk breaking his legs. Fate was listening to this remark the day I went off to the track in a big group of eight or nine with people like Alan Perkins, Martin Bastin and Robert Harding. Sure enough, Willie Thorne, Mr Lucky, felt the full impact as one of our group was catapulted into the tyres as we were messing about trying to knock each other off course. Kart and rider hit the tyres and both came smashing down on my legs as man and machine springboarded off the rubber wall. All I could hear was Gary's voice ... "You'll break your legs ... You'll break your legs."

I ended up in hospital with both of my legs in plaster. Gary came to visit me along with a local news cameraman who took one of those photos newspapers seem to love. There I was lying in bed, cue in hand, pretending to play a snooker shot off my legs, with Gary watching with a big grin on his face.

Soon afterwards, I was back at the club playing exhibitions. There were plenty of sponsored events in those days and I was sometimes paid to play two or three frames at these functions. The Post Office was holding one of their regular events and I agreed to play the exhibition with one leg still in plaster. That was one of the truly great moments of my career as our battered hero scored a 147 maximum to riotous applause.

During the 80s, sixteen clubs were opened in Leicester alone, as people copied our success. The snooker bubble has since burst and there are now only five or six scraping a living. The Willie Thorne

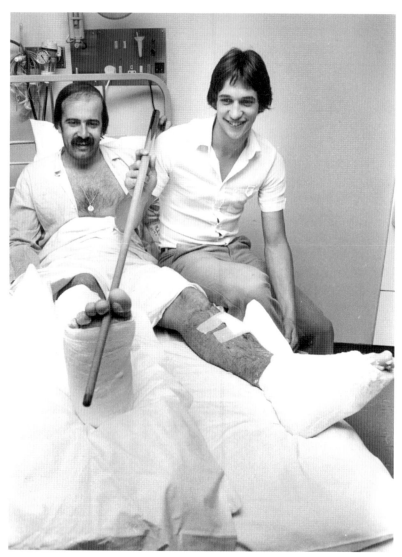

My go-karting exploits left me in hospital with both of my legs in plaster. Gary came to visit along with a local news cameraman who took one of those photos newspapers seem to love.

Snooker Centre carried on under my name and is still a nationally known venue. It is used for tournaments, especially at junior level, and seems to be doing well.

When I eventually sold my stake in the business in the late 90s, I did not sever my links completely. As part of the settlement, I was given a BMW Series 7 and I undertook to do four appearances a year for the next five years. I had not played anywhere else in Leicester during the boom years, in case I was accused of poaching business for the Willie Thorne Snooker Centre, so it was no great trial for me to keep up my connection with the club I'd founded. I carried on throughout the 90s, turning up at the centre and playing a couple of frames in an exhibition. The arrangement finished in 2001 but the Snooker Centre still continues to trade under my name. This doesn't give me the warmest of glows as they are basically making money out of my name and the effort that went into making my career.

I have lived in or near Leicester all my life, apart from an eight year period spent in Sheffield. Even during this spell in the 90s, I was often back in Leicester, calling in at the club to fulfil my playing commitments and visiting my family.

I have always stayed close to my mum. She has always been there for support both moral and financial throughout my life and I have always tried to give her back the affection she deserves. She was married to a difficult man and spent much of the time arguing with him. It was a relationship with an undercurrent of violence and I was often on the end of some physical punishment from my father. He was strict but he was always anxious to keep his children on the right path. He once saw my younger brother and me breaking into a hut at Anstey Nomads' football ground next to our house. He was incensed and punished us in his usual rough handed way before keeping the pair of us in the house for a fortnight.

I have such a collection of mixed feelings about my father. I could never bring myself to forgive him for what he did to my mother. The beatings and occasions when he locked her in the cellar are beyond the pale in a civilised society. Nowadays, his behaviour might well have led him into trouble with the law, but my mum, like a lot of women in such a situation, would probably have felt something of a failure if she'd gone down this route. She was prepared to stay with my father through the rough times, though she must have gone through hell.

I always cherish a lot of warm memories of my dad. I could never find fault with his generosity as he bought me all my sports equipment for football, cricket and snooker. To others, I suppose, I appeared to come from a family that was comfortably off. I certainly had the material comforts during my teenage years and also enjoyed some bonding moments with my dad. Apart from our forays to Gorse Hill for our hunting and shooting sessions, we used to go occasionally to Filbert Street to watch Leicester City. The Foxes had a series of good sides in the 60s with great players like Banks, Shilton and McLintock. They managed to get to a couple of Cup Finals and regularly finished in the top half of the old First Division. One incident will always stay in my memory from those Saturday afternoons. My dad was a massive man, well over 20 stone, with enormous strength, which he would use sometimes in a very controlled way. On this particular occasion, a bubble car tried to edge out from a side street into the slow moving queue we were in as we drove from the match. Without warning, Dad got out of the car and picked up the bubble car, driver and all and moved it out of our way. The poor bloke was speechless as my dad threatened him not to do it again.

Besides that attack of road rage, I only ever saw my dad behave violently outside the family on one other occasion. He was very good at controlling himself. The Shoulder of Mutton was a rough pub and there were times when Dad must have been sorely tempted to resort to violence. The only time I saw him crack was the time when a deliveryman had a go at Dad's enormous bulk. He flipped.

Those incidents apart, he was a very sociable, gregarious bloke, well liked by a lot of people. He started to drink quite heavily at our pub and elsewhere but he could never be classed as an alcoholic. Nevertheless I'm sure that one of the root causes of his violence towards my mum was drink. It was a relief, sometimes, when he would go off on his own on trips with the Licensed Victuallers. They would visit exotic places like Honk Kong and, while he was away, life was far more peaceful.

My mother always tended to put me on a pedestal, whereas my dad always felt the need to put me under one. He often came to watch me play in tournaments but was always hard on me and over-critical. I really resented this carping because I just didn't rate my dad's knowledge of the game. He was a hopeless player.

As I rose through the amateur ranks and then in the professional game, Leicester became a magnet for a number of snooker players. I was known in snooker circles as the national champion in my age group and I was also the son of a publican who had a lot of fairly cheap accommodation available in our massive pub. We had nine bedrooms as well as my practice room, so it was natural for players from the snooker world to come and stay with us. As I mentioned earlier, Higgins had lodged with us in 1972 and my dad was always inviting foreign players to stay. We saw a lot of Cliff Thorburn, Jimmy van Rensburg, whom I'd met in South Africa, Silvio Francisco and Bill Werbenuik. They gravitated to Leicester partly because they knew me and partly because of the growing reputation of the Snooker Centre which we had opened recently. They were trying to qualify for tournaments and break into the circuit in Britain and at the time, they just couldn't afford the prices of hotels.

The big man stayed with us for six months while we were living in Tudor Road and we were great pals. He was one of those players people still associate with the boom years. His size and those figure hugging suits in blues and silvers are etched on everyone's memory, just as is his appearance in the televised maximum break put together by Cliff. Bill was playing in the game on the other side of the screen as the break built up towards its climax. The Grinder moved on to the colours as Bill's huge frame suddenly appeared in the camera shot over Cliff's shoulder, looking like a naughty peeping tom. It was such a great image, showing what a bond there was between us all in those days.

Having said that, it was such a shame that we eventually had a major falling out in the twilight of Bill's career. Perhaps he was desperate for money but I couldn't really forgive him for selling his story to the *News of the World* for £10,000. He dished out the dirt on several players including Jimmy White, Higgins and myself. He accused me of owing him money when, in fact, the reverse was the case. He left immediately for Canada when the article appeared and, although he came back in 1991 and the following year, I never met him to talk to again. He died in 2002, so I was never able to straighten out our relationship.

Snooker became the focus for so much of my social life. I had obviously built up my circle of racing pals through my association with Osborne's and I still saw them from time to time at tournaments. One of the regulars at the old billiards hall was Barry Lineker who ran a greengrocer's stall on Leicester market. I used to play a card game called 'Kalookie' at a regular Wednesday night school at Barry's house. It was here that I first came into contact with Barry's son, Gary, who was 15 and had just started playing for the Leicester City junior sides. Gary was six years younger than me but we became good friends at a time when we were trying to make the breakthrough in our very different sports.

I frequently accompanied his family to watch him in the early 80s as he tried to make the big breakthrough. It is so exciting to watch somebody who you know really well, doing something at the top level on a very public stage. He'd made his debut as a winger on New Year's Day, 1979, when he was only 18 but he was then in and out of the side until they realised that his best position was not out wide but down the middle, where his amazing pace could be put to better use. We followed him all over the place in his early career, trying to give him that support which I know from personal experience is so vital to a player's self-confidence. I remember driving all the way down the M5 to Exeter with the tribe of Linekers to watch him make his FA Cup debut. He'd phoned to say he was in the side but we realised that, as the team ran out on to the pitch, there had been a last minute change of plan. It's a long way from Exeter to Leicester ...

It didn't matter about those early frustrations because we were to see a great deal of him as he established himself in the Leicester first team. At first, he found it difficult to make a big impact, almost the mirror image of the way my snooker career was proceeding. However, in the 1981-82 season he completed his breakthrough as Leicester's centre forward; ending up as top scorer, a position he was to hold for the next four seasons. It was great to watch him

Celebrating another win with Captain John and Racing Raymond.

come through that difficult early spell after a series of false dawns and such a thrill to see him wave to our little group in the stand at the start of each game and after every goal celebration.

Gary was quite a good snooker player and was always saying how much he envied me and that he would love to be a snooker player. He was earning very little in those days as a young pro, at a time when snooker players were getting £40,000 for winning a tournament. A lot of soccer pros played the game in those days and some, like Steve Ogrizovic and Andy Townsend, played snooker to a very decent standard. Snooker became footballers' preferred spare time sport, a position now occupied by golf, and it was never a surprise to see audiences at big events peppered with some of the game's glitterati.

Gary lacked the ability to become a pro snooker player but he reached that standard below the top level where he was just too good for the local league circuit. He would practise for as much as six hours a day when training was finished and became totally obsessed with raising his standard. I coached him and practised with him most days after the Snooker Centre had opened and he gradually developed a pro's break-building game. Though he only had a good amateur's ability, Gary could score heavily and was capable of century breaks. He's managed 15 centuries and a highest break of 134. I played him countless times during the 80s and he was always able to take one frame off me in every ten on the few occasions when we played off even.

He has given up the game now and has not played regularly since he went to Spain in 1986 to play for Barcelona. Nowadays he would probably struggle to get a break of 20. He is just too busy with his broadcasting work to put in the essential practice time. Typically, Gary has turned his attention to a new sporting obsession, golf. He was a 14-handicapper but in recent years, thanks to living near the sixth tee at Sunningdale and a series of lessons to remodel his swing, he now plays off four. Anyone who has played golf will realise what fantastic progress this is and it is a testament to his natural sporting ability and his desire to make the best of that ability.

The Linekers were regulars at the Willie Thorne Snooker Centre and I played Gary regularly in those days as my career was starting to take a turn for the better. I was obsessed with making 147 breaks and Gary was gaining the reputation of having more maximum 147 breaks against him than any other man on earth!. I have always loved the break-building aspect of the game. It is what sets it apart from any of the other table games and takes it to the level of problem solving. The problems change from frame to frame but there is a wonderful feeling you get every time you finish a maximum. You know that you have been in complete control of the balls and the scoreboard confirms the fact, in no uncertain terms, that you have achieved perfection.

In total, I have made 189 maximum breaks, probably double the amount of any other player but only one of those was achieved in tournament play. I did that in the UK Championships at Preston and it was the only time I managed to focus successfully and use the ability I knew I had. I have managed 37 other 147s in exhibition play when I have been far more relaxed and self confident.

Nevertheless, the nickname, Maximum Man, has stuck after all these years. David James, a local businessman saw my signature on a cheque I'd written for him. I don't know whether he was surprised that I could write or that he just loved the stylish flourish but he asked me if he could use the signature to endorse a line of socks he was marketing. Recently, he signed me up to promote a range of underwear predictably, and unsubtly, called Big Willie – Maximum Man Boxer Shorts.

My confidence grew as the 80s progressed and I was now firmly rooted in the world's top 16. Gary came to many of my tournaments and I was supporting Leicester City regularly. Soon, he became one of the hottest properties in English football and was transferred to Everton, the English Champions, in 1985, for £800,000. This was a huge sum in those days for someone who had only just received his first international cap and one which baffled Mrs Thatcher who, at the time, was leading enquiries about the ills of football after the Heysel disaster.

I became an avid follower of Everton for the 1985-86 season as Gary's career reached new heights. I used to go up to Tarleton, near Ormskirk, to pick him up and take him to the ground whenever I was free. I hadn't done a great deal of soccer gambling at this stage but I just had a hunch that I was on to something big that season. Professionally I was on a roll and so was Gary. I'd been asked early in 1985 what my hopes were for the New Year. My first major and Gary's first England cap was my answer and my wishes came true.

I was rolling in money and so a bet of two grand for Everton to win the FA Cup in 1986 was a modest one, almost restrained by my standards. The bet was placed in January at the third round stage and I forgot about it until the following May, by which time Everton had reached the all-Merseyside final to play Liverpool. I was on a run and sensed that there was a big touch on the cards. I wrapped a lot of money around the final with a couple of grand going on at 9/2 for Gary to be the first goalscorer. He had just been made Footballer of the Year, was about to go off to Mexico to play in the World Cup and was on top of his game. Just to make things even more interesting, another four grand was placed on Everton winning at half time and full time.

You wouldn't have been surprised to see me out of my seat, punching the air when Gary outpaced Alan Hansen through the centre as he ran on to Reid's pass, played the ball against Grobbelaar before clipping the rebound into the net – first leg completed.

The score was still 1-0 as the referee blew for half time. Second win achieved. At the start of the second half, I realised I had £150,000 riding on the outcome of 45 minutes of football. Then in stepped Ian Rush. An equaliser and that awful, doomed sick feeling. A great save by Bruce was followed by a goal by Johnston before Rush wrapped the game up with six minutes to go. At half time, it had been impossible to shut me up: now I was speechless, realising what a massive amount of money I had just missed. I didn't need the money. I'd won enough on the Lineker bet to cover my outlay on all of the bets. I wasn't on the chase but the crucial realisation was that I'd just missed out on that amazing buzz you get when your daring is rewarded and the bookies are beaten.

After that game, Gary was transferred to Barcelona for £2 million. I managed to get over and see him play a few times at the Nou Camp. That was an amazing experience, watching your best friend play on such a famous world stage and remembering those days, only a few years earlier, when he couldn't get into the Leicester side on a regular basis.

When he returned to England after his time in Spain to play for Tottenham, I saw a lot more of him. The first time I took him from his place in St John's Wood to White Hart Lane, he scored a hat trick. I took him there at least ten times and every time he scored at least once. On those car journeys, we would just chat about this and that, hardly ever mentioning the day's game. Needless to say, I didn't draw on my playing career with Anstey Martin school team to pass on tips and advice to a man who was England's record goal scorer and winner of the Golden Boot for the highest goals total in the 1986 World Cup.

I am still very close to Gary after all these years and, on average, I will still see him about once a month. He's moved away from Leicester but I still strongly associate him with the city. He's revered throughout the place and has been made a Freeman of the City. One of the stands at the new Walker's Stadium bears his name. He has an Honorary Masters Degree at the University and has been associated with the advertising campaigns of one of the city's biggest firms, Walker's Crisps. He was also a leading figure in the rescue attempts to stop Leicester City from going out of business and I know he still sees himself as a real Leicester man.

He's been a great mate over the last 25 years. We've shared some fantastic times together and we've also had some trials where we've needed each other's support. I was there for him when his son, George, was diagnosed with leukaemia. He was completely distraught and in tears when he broke the news to me. He would have exchanged everything that he had achieved in life for the health of his family. Gary has been there for me too in times of need. He is just a genuinely nice guy and someone you can always rely on for support and, boy, at times I've needed it in the last few years, when gambling has reared its ugly head and driven me close to the edge.

My brother Malcolm and me getting acquainted with the gee-gees.

chapter seven
THE HORSES

There are two types of gambler, the action gambler and the one who gambles to escape from problems. When I first started gambling it was part of my social life; something that was a natural activity in our group at Osborne's. We would bet on games of snooker but this was just wagering to benefit from your own skill at the table. People would come in and put their 50 pences on the table and sometimes a game would attract people who might bet amongst themselves on the outcome. It was all fairly low level betting but there was a gambling culture that made it so easy to gravitate into a much heavier form of the vice. I am not excusing myself: I am just trying to show how my environment could nurture my weaknesses. There was the Coral's betting shop just two doors down from Osborne's, so while you were between games it was natural to nip out and place your bet on whichever horse you fancied.

I got this bug of gambling when I was only 15 or 16 and it was largely due to the snooker environment I was operating in. Perhaps, though that's not being really truthful to myself, I would never have become a gambler if I'd not gone down to Osborne's. Perhaps if I'd not fallen in with Racing Raymond, I would not have become so enmeshed in horse racing and gambling, though when I read that back to myself, I realise that's not really fair to one of my best friends. Basically, it's very difficult to resist the attraction of horse race betting when you are surrounded by people who are backing horses. The buzz I discovered from standing in a betting shop and cheering on my horse was wonderful.

As I started going to the races with Racing Raymond, I became even more immersed in the sport and in gambling. I started to meet more and more people who were professional gamblers with a great deal of knowledge and a network of contacts within the racing world. All the time, I was building up a fund of knowledge and, like the classic action gambler I was, I reached the stage very quickly where I thought of the whole process as a game of skill. So, when I won with a big bet on the horses, it was an unbelievable feeling – so difficult to describe to a non-gambler. It's not about winning the money: it's about beating the system, winning a game. The money would become meaningless when you have a series of winners on a streak. The money, even in bundles of fivers, becomes unreal, almost like monopoly money. When you're winning, as the racing phrase goes, money is two bob a bucketful.

Just as it was at Osborne's, going to a race meeting was always great socially. Besides all the regulars in Racing Raymond's team, I met so many characters in the bookmaking fraternity and came into contact with professional gamblers like Ginger Steve and Micky Fletcher who have made gambling their job. Ginger had a fantastic knowledge of form and, more importantly, he had a lot of contacts inside the game. When I was gambling alongside people like this, it just made me more confident of my chances of winning big.

As time went by, I became more of a face as I moved up the snooker rankings. I built up a whole network of contacts with trainers and jockeys. A friend of mine, Steve McNamara, opened up a snooker centre in Newmarket in the early 80s. I gave him a few quid to get my name on the club and I helped him with the process of getting a licence and contacting suppliers.

So here I was in the capital of English flat racing, meeting trainers such as Henry Cecil and picking up tips on the form of horses at their yards ... or at least I chose to believe what they said. You would hear trainers dodging the issue when you asked about the condition of their horses. I have always wondered why trainers are never sure whether their horse is 100 per cent fit. How can stables say sometimes that the horse needs the run? How can they make this sort of judgement when they can see how the horse is performing on the gallops every day? The trouble for the gambler is to be able to sift out all the outrageous claims by stables and owners about the quality and chances of their horse. It becomes so difficult to assess a horse's chance and to forecast whether the animal was trying its best. A difficult conundrum to solve and one which has been complicated by jockeys deliberately holding back horses in a race to build up the odds for their next run. The recent exposé on television of crooked dealings in the sport didn't tell me anything I didn't know already but I still believe that, today, horse racing is straighter than it has ever been.

I hadn't been in Newmarket for very long when I was approached by John Wright, one of the partners in the snooker club with a tip from a trainer about a horse called Willie's Right On Cue. I watched it two or three times and then was given the tip to put a pile on when it was to appear at Sandown. I was able to get 16/1 at an ante-post price and put three grand on it. News filtered out and, by the start of the race, it had dropped down to 7/1, not that it mattered to me as the horse won and I collected nearly fifty grand. Newmarket was my kind of town ...

All action gamblers experience this stage of excitement and elation, usually bound up with a big win. It leads you to putting large sums on bets, just to maintain that level of excitement. The buzz can come at much lower levels of betting, especially if you are with friends and you are all using the same tip. I have been racing with John Virgo, snooker player, television host and general good bloke. He had lots of connections in the racing game, like so many of us and one of John's pals, Walter Swinburn, was to give us a tip on a horse at Sandown. Walter was riding a horse called Widdad which he reckoned was a certainty at 9/2, so we made a decent £400 bet for a win.

We were quite well known by this stage and decided to try the Members' Stand for the first time. For people who have never been racing, this area is a definite cut above the Tattersalls and Silver Ring stands and the entrance fee reflects the quality of the facilities, the view of the winning post and, some would say, the wealth of the clientèle.

As the field hit the home straight, Widdard was rolling all over the place as Walter struggled to straighten him. Instinctively, the pair of us started screaming and shouting, hoping that Walter, who was four furlongs away, could hear us. It worked - honest! With just one furlong to go, Widdard hit the front. The noise from the pair of us had built up to such a pitch that the lady in front turned on us. She was obviously well-heeled, dripping in furs and expensive jewellry and was not used to such an outburst of enthusiasm in the rather genteel surroundings of the Members' stand. She gave us a withering look and, in that awful accent of toff society, said, "Really! Snooker players should not be allowed in the Members' Stand," John, without taking his eyes off the race, said, "Look, love, you've got your fortune. We're still trying to get ours."

Getting tips and winning large amounts gives you a great kick but an even greater high comes from owning your own horses. In the 80s, I went into partnership a few times with Mel Smith, the comedian, and my professional gambler friend, Ginger Steve. Through the racing grapevine, Ginger heard of a horse being touted for sale by Cathy Lloyd-Jones. Racing is full of trainers who are trying to find owners to keep their stables full and profitable. I was instructed by the others to go up to North Wales to have a look at the horse, called Treasure's Jubilee, with a view to us buying it. The horse was out of action at that moment and wouldn't be fit for some time but Ginger had the hunch that it was the ideal material for us to engineer a major betting coup.

Cathy's yard was perfect for us. She had a stable with a small string of only ten horses and, as it was in North Wales, it meant that it was away from the hotbeds of racing and the rumour mill that can play havoc with the process of getting the best price for your horse.

I knew the background details of the horse when I went over to the stables. Treasure's Jubilee had won the previous season but it had picked up an injury and had not run now for over a year. I knew from the form books that the horse had only won twice in its entire career but Cathy had convinced Steve it had masses of potential, though it was suffering from a septic leg at the moment. Even when armed with all this information, I wasn't prepared for the shock when I first saw the horse. I can still remember walking through the yard as Treasure's Jubilee was being walked into its loose box.

My first reaction was to bite my tongue but my amazement got the better of me. "You're pulling my leg, aren't you, Cathy? It's on its way to the knacker's yard, surely." I didn't think I had seen anything uglier than Bill Werbenuik but this horse took the prize. It had a hole in its leg and lots of skin damage that couldn't disguise the extent of the infection and this just added to its forlorn appearance. But Cathy was adamant that the horse had genuine class and assured us that it would be a good buy. She was insistent that it had a fair amount of ability and, with its long absence from the track, it would be certain to start its next race at a really good price.

Curiously, by the time I'd left the yard I was convinced we were on to a winner. I already owned a couple of horses with Mel and Ginger but now had the job of convincing them that the investment of the £5,000 we'd negotiated with Cathy would be a good price. They agreed once I had convinced them that there was the real chance of a major coup. Ginger was very studied and calculating when it came to horses and betting and he now set about preparing for the big one. Typically, he drove up a few times to North Wales to watch the horse on the gallops before he was convinced that the time was right.

Treasure's Jubilee was eventually entered in a hurdle race at Ludlow over two miles. Martin Pipe had an odds-on favourite in the race which seemed to be attracting lots of money, as the price was shortening even further. By the morning of the race, I'd managed to put over £12,000 on the horse at various bookmakers across the country. I used the network of contacts that I pulled in whenever I wanted to put a lot money on a certainty and not attract the kind of attention that could bring the price down. Because I was earning good money at the time, the potential loss was not going to ruin me financially. Nonetheless, we decided to keep the horse in Cathy's name for the race, as you tend to find that celebrity names attract a bit of extra betting, which will then impact on the starting price.

I was so excited on the morning of the race that I decided to go down to the track rather than just wait in at home watching Ceefax. I'd been told by Steve to stay clear of Ludlow but the attraction of seeing this horse win was too much for me. It's a two-hour drive across the country from Leicester to Ludlow but the entire journey just slipped by as my mind raced.

By the time I arrived at the course, the first race was over. I was spotted straightaway by Micky Fletcher, the Asparagus Kid, as I walked to the stands. "What are you doing here?", he shouted after me. I rushed away but was followed by one of the Kid's men to see what I was up to. They knew I was there for a bet, so I realised that I would have to be very careful that afternoon with my pattern of bets.

Ludlow is a very pretty racecourse with a fantastic view of the entire course from the stands. The horses are never out of sight and the long, finishing straight is easily visible along its entire length for everybody at the meeting. My original intention was to go just to watch the race but I found it impossible to resist the temptation of betting. There were only six horses in the race and I started getting my doubts when I saw a lot of course money being laid on the favourite. It looked as if it was going to start at 4/6 whilst Treasure's Jubilee was out at 12/1. I was tempted to put a large bet on the horse but in the end I limited myself to a modest £100 bet.

Just to reassure myself, I went down from the stands and crossed the track to the parade ring to give our horse my final inspection. Cathy was there, as she was still the registered owner, and I managed to have a quick chat before the horses left. She just repeated what she'd told me at the yard. She knew it was a good horse because she used to ride it herself at the stables. "He may be ugly but look at him today. He's a certainty."

I got back across the course just before they closed the crossing gate and went straight to the bookies' area. Treasure's Jubilee had now hardened to 8/1 but this was still an excellent price for us to complete the coup. It had shown some ability earlier in its career but, given its lack of racing, and the fact it was from a small trainer's yard, we were not surprised by the size of its starting price. If it had been trained by somebody like Fred Winter, we would have had to settle for 3/1.

I climbed up into the magnificent stands for the start of the race. The Victorian building is listed and from the open area at the top there is a great view of the course and its wonderful setting, with the Welsh hills in the background.

At Ludlow, there is a long sloping section with no fences or hurdles before the horses hit the home straight. A large number of races are decided in this section before the horses hit the final four furlongs to the winning post. In the first mile, Martin Pipe's horse had shot into a 20-length lead as all his horses did in those days. Sure enough, just as Cathy had said, Treasure's Jubilee was showing his class as it worked its way through the field and moved into contention just as they turned into the home straight with three hurdles to jump. Two out and it hit the front and I realised we'd won. It probably lasted less than a minute but that final stretch to the line was mind blowing. I'd won £100,000 and I'd beaten the system. I'd wanted to scream myself stupid all the way down that final half mile but I managed to keep quiet, even though it was the most exhilarating feeling I've ever had on a racecourse. It was like doing something crooked and yet it wasn't: it was all completely above board and the system had been defeated.

I went over to the rail to pick up my winnings and somebody asked me why I had gone for it when it didn't have any form. I hoped they believed me when I came out with the glib answer that I'd just fancied it. I didn't really care and tried to keep up the Willie Thorne façade that everyone expected of me at the tracks. I made my way across to stable area where Cathy was just loading up our star act. She was obviously delighted, as a small stable doesn't get many long odds wins in a season, and all the hard work had paid off. She'd made a bit on the race and I had over a thousand pounds in my pocket but it was nothing compared to the pile that was flooding into my bank account as I meandered back to Leicester.

Cathy later closed the yard and went on to do other things. Treasure's Jubilee only lasted another year in training and didn't win another race. It had given me a wonderful moment in racing, so I was not too bothered or sentimental about its later form. I still had other horses to keep my interest going, but none of them ever gave me another a win on the scale of that amazing afternoon at Ludlow.

I had a handful of other substantial wins in what, I suppose, I could call the winning phase of my gambling addiction. In the mid-80s, I reached the final of the Benson and Hedges tournament in Ireland two years on the trot. I'd backed myself right through from the first round and had won nearly £40,000 by the time I was due to meet Steve Davis in the final. Not content with that buzz, I had also placed a considerable number of large bets during the week on horses on the strength of some reliable tips. Fortunately for me, Ireland had no Sunday opening for betting shops. I say fortunately because, without this regulation, I would have done something really stupid and risked my racing winnings on betting to beat Davis. I lost the final but I went home with £40,000 from my snooker bets,

£60,000 from my racing exploits and, of course, the runner up's prize which was more than £25,000. One hundred and twenty-five thousand pounds for a week's work and most of it tax free!

I flew back to Manchester with practically all of my winnings stuffed inside the lining of my coat. When I arrived at Dennis Taylor's house, I spread it all out on the floor to count it. The amount didn't mean anything to me. I was actually staying with the Silver Fox and so I asked him if he needed any cash as a loan. The £7,000 I gave him to buy a dining room suite was a convenient way of getting rid of some of the enormous bulk I'd brought back from Ireland.

As I've said before, wins on this scale are fairly meaningless in terms of money. Admittedly, there would be a fair old spending spree going on afterwards but I had developed a habit of hiding the bulk of any winnings in an effort to conceal from my wife the extent of my gambling exploits. This is a classic symptom of the problem gambler, the lying and the deceit. It seems funny now, but I can remember wearing a Crombie coat when I went racing and using it to conceal my winnings. At one Ascot meeting, I won over £40,000, in the days when you could only get £20, £10, and £5 notes. This huge stash of readies was stuffed into the pockets and through rips in the coat's lining, so that when I got home, I looked like the Michelin man. Then, in what had become a ritual, I would take it out and spread it over the carpet to count it with a wide grin across my face.

We had other horses in later years as the money from snooker kept on flooding in. I bought some like Maximum Man on my own after being approached by trainer, 'Spitting' Mick Easterby, who offered me a quality horse several classes above Treasure's Jubilee. After a great deal of bantering and bargaining, I told him I'd take the horse but with the proviso that he would give me a really hot tip sometime in the future. I bumped into Mick at a Leicester meeting soon afterwards and, as luck would have it, he gave me a tip for Wetherby the following day. I put £10,000 on it at 2/1 and it came up trumps.

Maximum Man was mine and I now had the flash status symbol of a horse with a personalised number plate, my nickname. Six months later, I was back to Spitting Mick to tell him I could not afford to keep him any longer. It hadn't won and in addition, events in my betting life were suddenly forcing my hand. I had hit a losing streak and money was just draining away. There are so many highs and lows in gambling and I was living such a high earning life that the extent of my losses did not immediately hit home. I was probably earning over 300 grand a year and yet I had the mind set to go out and try and win another quarter of a million pounds on top of this from gambling. It was reckless and silly but I needed the buzz.

As a high earner, I could get a lot of credit from bookmakers. It was just too easy to pick up a telephone and place a large bet. The amount I would recite to the clerk wasn't real money, it was just a set of words which had no relationship to value. I might have had a greater grasp of the reality of my financial situation if I had had to get the money out my back pocket but I was now in the position where I could bet and bet until I won. I may have started some days with the intention of having just one big bet but, because I was an action gambler craving the excitement of winning, I 'd be looking for a tip that would get me back on an even keel straightaway. If only I had had the ability and strength of someone like Ginger Steve to keep to a strategy. If only…

Cliff Thorburn celebrates making the first televised 147 break, with David Vine on the left and BBC producer Nick Hunter behind.

chapter eight
POCKET MONEY

Big money was always difficult to win, even during my heyday. Betting on snooker has only really developed in recent years, as has been the case with a lot of sports betting. The money in the 70s and 80s could only be earned by backing yourself.

Snooker was how I got into gambling. As an amateur, I was earning a lot of money from the game, sometimes as much as £20,000 for a single challenge match. We used to play for similar amounts when I turned pro but that usually took the form of practice matches behind closed doors. I played with Jimmy White on many occasions in the 80s when I lived in Sheffield.

Jimmy used to come up the week before the World Championships and we'd play each other over eleven frames for a modest side bet. In all those games, Jimmy never beat me but it was rather a hollow victory as that always seemed to be my peak. He'd go on to the finals or the semis, while I was destined to reach the quarter-finals on only two occasions. So, as serious as we tried to make it, those practice games were no substitute for the challenge of match play.

I had been able to win a fair amount in the 70s while I was still in Leicester. I used to play a guy from Birmingham called 'Bob the Butcher' at Osborne's. He ran one of the halls in that city and was quite a good player but I had to give him a 40 start. He could play one-handed, holding the cue like a pencil and, even using this bizarre technique, he was capable of breaks of 20 or 30. He could control the cue ball in a whole variety of ways, even screw shots. Despite his technical ability, I was able to make quite a bit of money off him because I was virtually unbeatable at the time. We played a variety of different formats – using the rest, playing with the long cue and giving starts, just to spice things up.

A whole host of players came across from Birmingham to challenge me. People like Les Adams, Lol Roberts, Stan Bate and

Josh Little were good players but I had to give them 14 or 21 points a frame to make the challenge more even. On one memorable occasion, six of them came over to Leicester and I had to play them one after another. At times, Osborne's resembled a barber's shop with a string of Brummies lined up to play me. They were a great bunch of blokes and we all got on very well. I saw them a lot over an eight-year period and I suppose that in that time I must have made more than £20,000 off them from our regular challenge matches.

It was quite a nice way to earn a few extra pounds. I was only ever beaten once at Osborne's, by Patsy Fagan, so my income was fairly consistent, quite unlike the highs and lows of horse race gambling. Occasionally, I won a really big stake, like my £28,000 victory over an enthusiastic amateur called Jack the Aussie. I met him when he had come over to England after selling his business in Australia. He was trying to make a living as a professional gambler and snooker hall hustler. Jack got in touch with me as he had heard that I was someone who played and loved to bet. He challenged me to play at a Hammersmith billiard hall. I had heard through the grapevine that he was a hopeless player but he was someone who had the knack of potting a red and a colour and then leaving the next red safe. I gave him what seems like an unbeatable start of 82 in every frame we played and stupidly agreed to have no time limit on the match. Normally a match would be the best of 11 frames, which meant that even the tightest of matches would last three hours at the most.

Jack turned up with his clothes and slippers in a little sports bag. I had been told that he was travelling around the country with a another bag – a little paper one full of readies. Sure enough, and without any ceremony, he plonked it on the table. We were playing for £2,000 a frame and as I had been told he had about £15,000, I reckoned it would be a quick job to clear him out.

He really was a crap player but I made the mistake of trying too many difficult shots. If I'd played tighter and given him fewer opportunities, the game would have been over in no time. As it was, the match dragged on and on. There was Jack getting the occasional colour with his appalling technique, flicking his cue up in the air, Zorro-like, after every shot.

Eventually, I managed to get £12,000 in front and casually went over to check the paper bag. Even my furtive little glance made me realise that he'd actually brought far more than £15,000. He must have been on a good run because it looked as if there was double that amount stuffed into the bag. The pound signs now started rolling around my eyes, even though I was knackered. To cut a long game short, let me just say that I began to grind my way towards the big prize. It was so difficult for me to beat the handicap we'd agreed to because I had to score at least 100 points in every frame. Twenty-six hours after we started, I managed to win the final £2,000 and left to drive up the M1 for home. Ten miles up the motorway, exhaustion hit me and I handed the wheel to someone else and collapsed on the back seat.

One of the easiest wins from snooker betting was from that involvement with *Pot Black*. I could have been far greedier betting on matches which I had seen being played months earlier. I probably made £2,000 on those bets but it could so easily have been more. It was cheating in a sense, but I had no qualms about taking money from bookmakers who had not done their homework on television broadcasting. I drew the line under cheating when I was a player.

You always hear whispers in snooker about match fixing but the only time we have ever been certain were in the matches involving the Franciscos, Peter and Silvino, in the 80s. A lot of big money was laid illegally in Ireland on matches in Britain at a time when betting tax was ten per cent. Peter Francisco was playing a match against Jimmy White. Big money had gone on a 10-2 scoreline and at 10.30 in the morning, as the match resumed, there was a strong smell that this was going to be the final score. Jimmy realised this but there was nothing he could do about it as the match petered out to its foregone conclusion. Francisco was found out and, for the sake of a few quid, he had thrown away a decent career. Every pro would have told him not to be such a bloody idiot, especially as we were all aware of the damage it could do to the squeaky clean image of our sport and our livelihoods. He was given a swingeing five-year ban by the authorities, leaving nobody in any doubt of the will to nip any chance of a repeat firmly in the bud.

Me with Linda Lusardi on the circuit. I've always been a stickler for formal dress.

chapter nine
RAISING THE STAKES

I had met a guy called Richard Olsen in my days at Osborne's. He was a massive man weighing at least 25 stone and was larger than life in more than the obvious way. He played snooker but his claim to fame lay in the board game, backgammon. He attracted hardly any publicity, which was odd, as Richard was, at one time, World Champion. He won tournaments in Birmingham, which in the 80s was something of a hot bed for the game, as was Crockford's in London. It was so big, even ten years ago, that crowds of up to a 100 would watch some of the big games with everybody following a strict dress code.

Imagine Richard's surprise when I phoned to invite him to Pontin's holiday camp for a match. I used to love going to the camp in Prestatyn to play in the tournament immediately after the Embassy World Championship in Sheffield. I won the trophy a couple of times, so naturally I've got a soft spot for the place. Richard obviously thought the place was a bit downmarket for him but, after I had convinced him over the phone that there was a lot of money to be earned, he appeared in an immaculate suit, handmade shirt and expensive shoes. He looked like a complete toff attracted by the smell of the easy money. Chinese Tony, the best backgammon player in Manchester, had come to Pontin's with the same idea and was winning quite a bit from punters from all over the country. I approached him with the chance of playing Richard for £100 a point, an offer that was too good to ignore. It was a great game, lasting virtually a whole day before Richard eventually clinched it to win £12,000. Naturally, I won a little on the side through betting on Richard.

One of the highlights was to come later when I went with Richard to the World Championship which was held in Monte Carlo. It was held in the casino, which was big enough to accommodate 200 players, all playing at once. The championship was divided into age categories – senior, intermediate and junior – with each group assigned a room in the building. The doors were left open, which meant that there was an amazing din from the rattling of hundreds of dice. Although Richard played well, he missed out on the championship. Nevertheless, we managed to win a few grand at the tables so the trip was paid for and the buzz and excitement of playing in the mecca of gambling, is a memory that never fades.

We came into contact with lots of very unusual people in those days of backgammon gambling. One of my contacts in the world of gambling was a guy called Curly Mick, whom I was able to use to set up a game between Richard and a professional gambler by the name of Harold Conister. Terms were agreed to play for the astronomical figure of £200 a point, a rate which meant that it would be possible to win £50,000 in next to no time.

Now Harold had a reputation as a very good trickster, a player capable of throwing dice almost to order. He was able to rattle one of the die in the cup whilst concealing the other in his palm. This meant he could reduce the odds from 17/1 to 5/1 every time he threw, as the die from his hand could be any number he chose. This match in Leicester was all very cloak and dagger, with Harold appearing under a pseudonym and the rest of us playing along with his subterfuge. He did not show it but he must have been thrown when it was suggested that I should be the one to shake the dice for him. He agreed, taking care not to blow his cover, as he had complete faith in his own tactical ability as a backgammon practitioner. In contrast, I was a bag of nerves but the strategy worked and, after a really long session, Richard won over £6,000.

Richard was also a very good card counter and brought his remarkable skill to the ace game, or blackjack. I was his stooge in the casinos and we quickly became so good that we were getting £50 a shoe. Richard was able to watch a shuffle and could often tell when a card was coming up. In these situations, he would go for the maximum bet of £500 per box, while it was my job as stooge to create a bit of a distraction by chatting everybody up as they sat round the table. I was quite well known by that time as a snooker player, so I could be the distracting presence necessary for Richard to win heavily. I didn't need the money, but it was such a great feeling beating the system, just as it was on the race track or when betting on snooker.

We usually won, however, and our success reached a level where places were banning us. I suppose that was fair enough, even though we were not guilty of anything illegal but I was a bit taken aback when Ladbrokes decided to ban me from my old stamping ground, the Barracuda on Baker Street. They had taken it over from the old owners and probably did not appreciate how long I'd been associated with the place. A couple of years later we had a blazing row when the dealer misheard a card/no card call. I was asked to leave and stormed out but, after an exchange of letters, an apology was made and I was reinstated. I was hurt because, despite all my weaknesses, I had never cheated in the arenas of gambling.

My reputation as a big gambler led to regular invitations to play cards for money. I was always able to hold back. It was different with horse racing because I always felt that I had a good chance of a big win using my contacts and knowledge of the sport. However, with poker and other card games where there was a lot of money to be earned, I knew I was a novice and would stand little chance against the experts. I sound almost sensible, don't I?

Casino betting was exciting and attractive but I only did a modest amount of betting on my own account. It was yet another one of the temptations that was thrown at me during the winning phase of my gambling career. Whenever I went to places like the Barracuda, I had the most fantastic treatment and I revelled in playing the big shot. My car would be parked for me as I pulled up outside the club. I'd then be taken by limousine to the theatre and out to dinner before being brought back to the club. With this level of complementary treatment, it would have been churlish to resist the temptation of various gambling games on offer. After the heady days working with Richard, I gambled at what I would call a social level. I would win perhaps £2,000 in a night but, more often than not, I would lose that amount. I believed my gambling was under control and was basically too lazy to learn how to win in casinos, relying too much on Richard.

We used to gamble with another real character known as the 'Chief'. Whenever I was in London, I used to see him at the

Barracuda, perhaps a couple of times per month. He was an arms dealer who, when I first met him, had bucketsful of money on him and was losing it at a remarkable rate, sometimes as much as £10,000 per night. However, when we teamed up with Richard, we turned the tide. It was so easy for Richard to know where the majority of aces were in a six pack shuffle. He always had this incredible skill of knowing exactly where three aces would appear.

Fortunately for me, in the period after Richard was banned, my losses were limited, not just by my own reluctance to gamble in an unskilled way, but for the more basic reason that in casinos you cannot get credit. Occasionally, it is true, I would lose £2,000 at the tables and, after going back to the hotel and sulking, I would come back with another £2,000. This rarely happened because I mainly went to casinos to enjoy the social buzz and bask in the limelight as a well-known sports personality. It is so easy and seductive to play the fame game but it did help me to build up my network of contacts and tipsters. I was not just addicted to gambling: I was addicted to the social whirl, the excitement of being in the public eye and, I suppose, the notoriety of being Willie Thorne, the gambling snooker star.

At this time, I was also a big spender and was generous to my friends, lending them money which I didn't always get back. If I think hard about it, I'm owed over £70,000 by various people but there's not much point brooding because I know I'll never be able to get any of it back from people who are skint.

I have known so many people who've lost everything through gambling. The people who I knew at Osborne's were all action gamblers, living life at the edge, always craving the excitement of betting. Brian Cakebread was a classic example from those days. He was a very good snooker player whose days would follow a fairly regular pattern. He would devote most mornings to playing snooker or billiards before spending the afternoon in the betting shop. He'd then be down to the dog track, at seven, before ending up in the casino for a few bets. He usually had enough adrenaline left to go on to a card school. Occasionally, Brian would win £5,000 but a lot of the time he was absolutely skint. When he asked me for a loan of £100 I always gave it to him, as amounts that size didn't make an appreciable difference and, more importantly, it was the kind of thing that was normal and natural to everyone in the betting and gambling world.

I certainly never resented it, as I owe a big debt to Brian. He made me into the player that I am – or was. He is a character, still following the same life style around the betting shops and snooker halls and still coaching players, just as he had done with me all those years ago.

chapter ten
LOSING IT

Problem gamblers always hit the losing phase after the initial winning period and run into real trouble even though they think their habit is under control. I always deluded myself that I could stop gambling whenever I wanted to but, in the late 80s, I never really felt the need to quit, even though I started on a very gradual decline which continued relentlessly for 18 months.

By this time, I was married and I had become devious enough to hide my losses from my wife. It was relatively simple to carry on this deceit, as my playing commitments took me away from home a great deal. My wife, Fiona, had lived with me for four years before we married in May 1985. She had lived through the good times with me and, although she realised that I gambled heavily, she was quite happy with our lot. She had witnessed the ritual often enough of me spreading bank notes all over our floor, as I returned from a successful trip to the racecourse. She could see those tangible fruits of victory, as well as all the other trappings of success that snooker had brought us. We lived in a beautiful house in Leicestershire, had expensive cars and could afford exotic holidays. When we eventually married, we had a really glitzy, showbiz wedding day. Gary was my best man and all the snooker fraternity was there, together with people from television like Dickie Davies and local sports stars like Alan Smith of Leicester City.

We married in Oadby, a village close to the racecourse in Leicester. It was all very glamorous, with crowds lining the streets as we drove in an open carriage to the church. The reception was held at the Hermitage, which was just across the road from the church and was run by an absolute gambling nutter. The food at the reception was going to cost £6,000, so I had handed over £2,000 to the manager in advance. I suppose most people in my situation would not have thought twice about this sort of transaction but, within two days, he'd decided to do a runner with my money. It wasn't the end of the world, as I was earning so much, but I did feel badly let down by a fellow gambler; but then, I suppose, you should expect these things when people are sucked into gambling and become desperate.

The big day wasn't spoiled by this deceit. The reception, which was held in a big marquee behind the Hermitage, was wonderful. A friend of mine, Jeff Ford, a country singer from Peterborough, wrote a song for me as a wedding present:

Willie Thorne – you were born with a snooker ball in your hand,
If you ever quit playing snooker,
I believe you could always join a band.
You do what you do
and you do it so well…

It was called the *King of the 147* and was played on television and radio during the Benson and Hedges tournament after I had made a big break. If I'd become World Champion, perhaps it would have been marketed and sold all over the place. *If* I'd become World Champion … Anyway, I've kept a copy and still think of it as a really kind gesture from Jeff on my wedding day.

In the August of 1985, Fiona gave birth to twins. I was at the height of my earning powers so I could easily provide for life's luxuries, including au pairs and nannies. However, I was away from home a great deal and was surrounded by all the temptations that come with hotel life. I was living the life of a celebrity and enjoying every minute of it but, I have to admit, that I don't look back at that period of serial liaisons with any great pride. I wasn't faithful but it was easy to cover up the truth from my wife.

My betting, too, could easily be covered up from Fiona, especially when there was lots of money coming in, but it became so much harder when I hit a losing streak.

When I was in one of those phases, I could still manage to put on a big front. Everybody thought I was just the same, always up for a laugh, always out for a good time. It gave me a strange kick at racecourses when people would follow me to the bookmakers to watch where I was putting my money. I played along, quite stupidly putting on far more than I originally intended, as it was easy at the racetrack to keep up this superficial jack-the-lad bonhomie and give everyone who didn't know me the impression that everything was fine.

The losing streak just got worse and worse. I would go through phases where I could lose £50,000 in a very short time. When this happens, the pressure really starts. When you're on a winning streak, you feel you cannot lose but once your luck changes, each bet is approached with a gut churning apprehension. By this time, I was on the classic downward spiral, lying about my gambling and my losses and then starting to borrow money secretively from my family and friends. I loathed this deception but I was getting more desperate, borrowing as much as £10,000 at a time. My line was always one of a promise to pay them back the following week as I was having a little bit of cash flow crisis. Often, I would only give back two grand and I'd be using the other eight grand to pay back somebody else or invest it on another horse. I've always tried to avoid lying but, when you're losing, you deceive everybody about how well you're doing, how much money you have and when you are going to repay loans. I suppose it's an act of betrayal but every problem gambler would understand that because they've done it themselves.

Some of my friends, like Gary, started to realise that I was getting into trouble and tried to persuade me to calm down. It was to no avail, because I was now in that phase of gambling called the chase. When you are in this phase of problem gambling, you start to take extraordinary risks, backing horses that have big prices, or investing stupid amounts on odds-on favourites. The whole aim in the chase is to win money quickly and in huge amounts. Remember, I was still a highly-ranked snooker player at this time but most of my days were spent thinking about my plight and how to come up with the big winner to turn everything around.

My gambling was becoming more and more secretive. It was easy for me at this time to milk my celebrity status and to open accounts with a whole host of firms. More damaging for me, however, was the realisation that these bookmakers would give me enormous amounts of credit, because I had played the big, successful gambler role so well and I had the skill and the time to move money around my different accounts. I had twelve accounts, at least, all of them with very different balance sheets. If I had a big win on one account, I would keep the money in that account building up brownie points for the future. When the account day came round on Monday, I would then switch that credit balance to another account where I was losing. I managed to keep all these balls in the air for months before things started to go badly wrong.

This phase was having a damaging effect on my marriage. Fiona became aware of the state of our finances and how close we were to bankruptcy. The mountain of bills coming into the house couldn't be paid. My betting accounts were being closed as word went round the betting community about my mounting debts. Victor Chandler was one of the first to warn me off but soon Tattersalls had been informed that Mr Thorne had not settled his debts with all of his bookmakers. Bankruptcy had a terrible stigma attached to it in the 80s. I had read about other people going bankrupt and could remember the kind of conversations I would join in, gossiping about their plight.

I was now entering the final phase of problem gambling – desperation. I found it harder to keep up the façade that everything was fine. My mood swings were making it more and more difficult for me to keep my temper at home, as I became increasingly irritable under the strain. My losses were mounting up but I still had this fantasy of having a really big win which I believed, quite naively, would cure everything at a stroke. As time ticked by, however, I started to believe deep down that I had reached the stage where I really couldn't win, no matter how good my tips were. Every time I picked up the phone to make a bet, I felt that fate was going to be the winner and I would be left backing the losing odds-on favourite. Yet, perversely, I carried on.

In some ways, I was shutting myself off from the people around me as I tried desperately to focus on the next day's bet as well as squeezing in some snooker practice. I was fortunate at this time in that I didn't need to practise a great deal to keep my game in reasonable nick when I wasn't in a tournament. I would sometimes go three or four days without going to a table and then would only need five hours' practice to get the touch going again.

During this terrible period, I avoided doing what our friend at the Hermitage had done. He'd stolen money from me but I was able to steer clear of this and any other illegal activities such as writing bad cheques. I may have been tempted but, at least I can reassure myself that I didn't sink that low.

Occasionally, during this really desperate phase, I did get some fleeting moments of success. I might even have had a brief winning streak which would have raised my hopes and altered my mood, but these runs were just blips on a relentless, downward slide. All they ever did for me was to give me false dawns, keep me gambling longer and running up even bigger debts.

Everything seemed to conspire against me during this desperate chase. I was in serious financial trouble in 1987 and realised that I would have to sell the house in Great Glen. We had a very large house on the road leading in to this village where another local boy, Gerry Dorsey (aka Englebert Humperdinck), also had a base. I put the house on the market for what was, in those days, the huge sum of £450,000 and was offered £400,000 within a day. My luck was running out, as along came the stock market crash which had a catastrophic effect on the property market. Three months later, the house was sold for £275,000, so in effect I'd lost £125,000, an amount that would have made all the difference in settling my accounts. I was now bankrupt.

The stability of the rest of my life took a terrible pounding at this time when Fiona found out about a relationship I'd been hiding from her and a lot of other people too. My marriage was suddenly over as I took the coward's way out by leaving her and the children to move to Sheffield to live with someone I'd been having an affair with for the previous 18 months. I thought of myself as a coward because I knew my world was about to collapse. I was going to lose my house, my solvency and, with it, my dignity. I ran away because I didn't want to face the music.

Even after all these years, I still have deep regrets about my actions in those fraught, confused days. I accept that things weren't great at home but I should have felt more of a responsibility to Fiona, who'd been a good wife and a fantastic mother to our twins and young daughter, Tahli. In so many ways, the break-up was inevitable, given the kind of life I'd led for the past ten years. Being away from home so much had put a great strain on our relationship.

Fiona hardly ever came to tournaments and it was very easy to have affairs. There were so many opportunities, going to night clubs and casinos, meeting women who were obviously attracted by celebrity, though hardly by good looks. When I was in a town for a week, it was just too tempting to ask someone out for a drink and some fun.

I behaved badly. I deceived my wife, keeping this part of my life really well hidden. I'd been able to keep her away from my affairs, just as I had been able to hide away my financial dealings from her. I was able to separate my post from hers, making certain she never saw my bookmakers' bills, especially those with huge debts of up to £20,000 against my name. I was only able to get away with this for so long before walking out.

At least I could salve some of my guilt by paying for a seven bedroomed house for her and the kids to move into once the sale of the house had gone through. When the settlement, as part of the bankruptcy repossession order, was agreed in court, I was left with a monthly maintenance bill of £1,068. There was a great sense of relief, as I felt that a chapter of my life behaving badly had come to an end and I could make a fresh start.

So, I went to live in Sheffield with my girlfriend, Denise. For the next three years, I had no bank account and no credit cards but I was still full of optimism despite the disasters of the previous two years. I was in love and was about to enjoy six of the best years of my life, living in a city I really liked. Through Denise I made a lot of new friends. We lived in her apartment which was really nice and close to the city centre. For the first few days after the affair unfolded, I was besieged by the tabloid press. I was in the *News of the World* again. 'Love Rat Willie Thorne Leaves Twins' ran the headline above a picture of Denise leaving the flat with me. It didn't do a lot for my mood but at least I could fall back on my experiences of my last brush with the Press. I liked seeing my picture in the papers when it played to my ego, showing pictures of Willie Thorne at the Races. This was all part of building-up an image and keeping my name in the public eye, with all its advantages when it came to negotiating appearance money at exhibitions and dinners. But when the Press pack are hounding you, it is a totally different experience, making you feel angry, resentful, and, more importantly, very depressed.

Tristan and Kieran welcome their new sister, Tahli.

Kieran, Tahli and Tristan.

chapter eleven
THE BRINK

After I first went bankrupt, it seemed impossible that I would put myself and those around me through the same pain again. As well as losing over £250,000, my marriage was over and I had lost regular contact with my children. I was determined to get my life back on an even keel and was optimistic about the future. I was still earning good money as a snooker player and I could afford to pay the alimony and child support, as well as enjoying a comfortable life style in Sheffield.

My betting was more under control, although I had reverted to the pattern of an archetypal action gambler. I was able to conceal my gambling and the extent of my losses from Denise, as I was away from the city much of the time. Denise had her own career in Sheffield, working for a menswear company and was unable to follow me to tournaments, or to the golf celebrity tournaments I was starting to attend at weekends. With all the bills being paid and living in a nice apartment, I suppose she didn't really have much cause for concern.

Although I can say that my gambling was more under control, I was still capable of betting four or five grand at a time and, with my contacts and expertise, I was capable of landing some big wins on the racetrack and through snooker.

Occasionally, I had some crazy bets like the John Parrott game, but I was still in control at that point in 1996. That big bet did drop me in trouble, briefly, but I was prepared for it. In some ways, it was a measured bet, because I'd done something similar in the days when I was a top eight player. My friend, Cliff Thorburn, was playing Steve Newberry in the Rothman's tournament at Reading. Steve was a decent player but way down the rankings compared with Cliff's top eight placing. It was not surprising that Thorburn was 1/5 in the betting and Steve was 9/2.

Cliff saw me before the match and was not his normal placid self.

He'd left his cue behind when he was packing the car before setting off for Reading and had only had the briefest of practices with a replacement that he'd borrowed from John Spencer. This was not the time for personal loyalty as I made preparations with my various contacts to get as much on Newberry as possible before the bookies suspected anything and suspended betting. Willie the Gambler now replaced Willie the Pal. I managed to get £10,000 on Newberry between 11am and 11.30. I'd also circulated my network of nutters from Osborne's and they too were in for a killing. The betting pattern was picked up by the betting firms but too late, as far as I was concerned. Steve won 5-0 and I picked up over £35,000. A good day and one which, I'm certain, affected my judgement that night, nine years later, in the Chinese restaurant in Motherwell.

As a gambler, you always remember the days when you beat the system: not just the size of your winnings but the buzz you get from discovering a certainty, following it through with a bet and then winning. You also remember the nearlys, the what ifs, the bad luck. The Parrott bet obviously fell into this category but there were two other calamities during the 90s that I often brood about.

I once had an each-way accumulator where I needed the final horse to win me £44,000. It was called Another Time, a 9/4 favourite in an eight-horse race and I only needed a place, first, second or third, to collect my jackpot. It was a good horse running in a handicap and everything seemed perfect as it hit the front. Then the Great God of Racing intervened – it fell on the flat! It was the only horse in the entire flat season to fall and, to make it even more unbearable for me, it went on to win its next three races and is still in training as a useful ten-year-old hurdler. Now that really was bad luck.

However, that disaster was topped when I had another multiple bet, this time in Scotland. I had backed three horses in £500 each-way doubles. I'd also used the same horses as the basis of three £500 each-way trebles. The first two horses won, leaving the final selection, Satterjack, with the responsibility of winning me £70,000. As it came into the straight, it was 15 lengths in front with just one more obstacle to clear. Over it went and with me screaming my head off like every self-respecting punter would, it cruised towards the line. With 15 yards to go the unthinkable and the unbelievable happened – its weight cloth fell off from below the saddle. That sort of thing happens every two years and meant that old Satterjack crossed the winning line miles in front but without the cloth that's needed in the weighing room. This was so galling because he'd run such a good race and was so much in the lead that you thought the jockey could have stopped the horse, dismounted, picked up the cloth and still been a comfortable winner.

It is that sort of bad luck that really makes the depression kick in. If those two bets had come off, it would have got me out of a terrible mess because I really needed the money. In both instances, I didn't lose a lot of money. I was just missing out on winning that elusive pile that I needed to settle my debts and turn my finances around. This is classic action betting, always looking for the big win that would settle the gambler's problems.

My relationship with Denise had foundered by this time. The demands placed on me to travel to tournaments proved to be the prime cause of our break up. We were gradually drifting apart, not because of my gambling this time but the small amount of time we actually spent together. We were well suited and had some happy times together but the temptations of life on the road and the basic fact that we were leading very different separate lives meant that it was inevitable that I would begin another affair.

I was at the World Championships in Sheffield, playing, doing some commentary work and helping out the sponsors with Dennis Taylor and John Virgo within the corporate hospitality area. Somebody mentioned that one of the promotions girls in another part of the Embassy suite was an ex-Miss Great Britain. "Hello", I thought to myself and went off to check out the scenery. Before I knew it, I was chatting away to her after I'd used one of my snooker/card tricks as an ice-breaker. I'd spread out a pack of cards face down across a snooker table before making a shot.

"What card were you thinking of?" Was my immortal opening line, but it did the trick.

Her name was Jill and, as luck would have it, the only reason she was working there with Embassy was that her friend had fallen ill and she had moved in as a last minute substitute. Perhaps it was

Sheffield was never a happy hunting ground in the Embassy World Championship ... until I met my beautiful wife, Jill.

fate, but I realised that this attractive woman was definitely a bit special. She told me over dinner that night that she'd left her husband that week. "That's handy!" I thought ...

We saw a lot of each other over the next fortnight and I realised that I was falling for her in a very big way. We carried on meeting for the next six or seven months as discreetly as possible and behind Denise's back. Sheffield is a big place but with the size of our social circle, it was inevitable that Denise would find out. Somebody told her what was going on and I was given an ultimatum of either choosing her and staying, or going. I realised that things had developed to such an extent with Jill that there was really no alternative but to leave.

I moved back to Thornton, just outside Leicester, to live with my mum. Jill and I continued a rather distant relationship for eight months with me commuting to her home in Stocksbridge just outside Sheffield. This arrangement continued until we decided to become an item and set up home together. By this time, I was starting to feel an economic pinch as my career was on a downward slope and my betting losses were giving me a real worry.

I had not hidden any of this from Jill. She knew that I was somebody who was always ducking and diving and who had a long history with the bookmaking fraternity. I was not quite bankrupt but money was rapidly getting tighter. Once again, I was approaching the desperate stage where I was having to borrow money from family and friends.

We found a house to move to in Leicestershire but we were having a lot of problems raising the £20,000 needed for the deposit. We still didn't have it the day before contracts were due to be exchanged but, at the last minute, one of Jill's family stepped in with a loan. I made assurances that it was only a short term deal and that I'd pay them back almost straightaway.

The house cost £175,000 and the monthly repayments of £800 put an enormous strain on my earnings as I also had to find £1,068 monthly alimony for my first wife. The fear of bankruptcy was always at the back of my mind, even though attitudes towards this parlous state were changing. The stigma attached to going bankrupt seemed to have softened. My first bankruptcy was a horrible experience which I wouldn't wish on anybody. I became slightly paranoid when the news first hit the papers, as I started to believe that everybody was talking about me. This had scarred me and, as my luck started to drain away along with my cash for the second time, I began to worry about the way my family and friends would see me. Would they all regard me as the idiot I felt that I was?

Tensions now started to mount as the months ticked by. I was still doing a balancing act with my domestic bills but to outsiders I looked as if I was rolling in money. In truth, my debts were so enormous that even if I was picking up five grand an appearance, the reality was that I was skint. Then came the threat of legal action and, somehow or other, I galvanised myself into another big effort of moving my money around from one creditor to another. The debt was paid off but I had created a lot of bad feeling.

There was a whole host of people I didn't want to let down at this stage. My mum had always been so supportive throughout my life, always giving me completely unconditional love. She could easily see through the brave face I was putting on in front of friends and everybody else I came into contact with. However, she couldn't see those dark moments of depression that I had in private. To Mum and everybody else, I was still Willie Thorne the joker, always up for a laugh and a giggle, somebody who didn't seem to have a care in the world. My mum was partly aware of my predicament and, after giving me a good telling off, was always prepared to lend me a couple of grand whenever I was in a tight spot. I always paid her back but I suppose that I was always afraid of the day when, perhaps, I couldn't.

My mum has been one of the rocks in my life. She did not have the easiest of marriages, as my father was, as I have mentioned earlier, not slow in using force to settle things within the family. My mother put her family's needs before her own. Dad used to drink and this made him even more volatile and added to the arguments my parents always seemed to be having. The money Mum and I made setting up the Willie Thorne Snooker Centre meant she was able to buy a bungalow in Thornton where she still lives to this day.

My parents' marriage was over when she moved out of the pub but their relationship still had a final chapter, which, to most people, would seem strange. We'd given Dad a job at the Snooker Centre but he drifted away to do other things. He tried his hand in the snooker business, setting up a place called the JW Thorne Snooker Centre. Looking back at the blazing rows they had had throughout my teenage years, I still find it unbelievable that my mother would take him back. He had lived with another woman at the Shoulder of Mutton yet, even after this and all the memories of unhappy times, she took him back when he suffered a couple of strokes, in the mid-90s, losing all control over his left arm. He couldn't drive anymore and he was feeling sorry for himself, so Mum let him stay with her in the bungalow.

He used to cry a lot whenever I made my duty visits to see him and found it increasingly difficult to talk as his speech became more and more slurred. Unable to string his ideas together and confined to a wheelchair, he became a rather pathetic figure. He would still have his good days, especially when he holidayed at West Runton, in Norfolk, in my mum's caravan during the summer months. He'd still get a kick out of things like his new powered wheelchair but the decline was steady and eventually he suffered a third stoke. He had to go into hospital and I slowly began to realise just how much he'd meant to my mother, despite all the bad times. While they were doing tests on him in hospital, he had his final fatal stroke.

My mum was still convinced that I could make it back to the top and I think she still believes it to this day. She has always been so proud of me and has always stood by me through my marriage break-up, the press scandals and the bankruptcy. Early on in her life she had been a dedicated churchgoer and she has always worked for others.

She is still my biggest fan and has always revelled in my celebrity. Mum will still introduce herself in restaurants as Willie Thorne's mother and loves it when people recognise me on the street. I have known her walk five yards behind me through Sheringham market, in Norfolk, so that she can watch the occasional person say, "It's him, isn't it?" She used to travel the length and breadth of the country to watch me play when I was younger. This has stopped now but she still loves asking me about crowd reactions and whether people still recognise me when I am doing the commentary at one of the big tournaments.

Her biggest strength is her amazing ability to think only of the future. She never dwells on the past, though she will bollock me now when I ask for the loan of a few quid. She has always been very careful with her money and has never been overdrawn in her life. When I trawl through my memories and try to work out why I have spent and wasted so much money on gambling, my mother's attitudes towards money present a strange conundrum. How can anybody with a mother like mine end up as a gambler? It wasn't in the genes and it certainly wasn't in the way my mother brought me up.

John Hayes was another person I was afraid of letting down. He was an old friend of mine from schooldays and had done various things until we bumped into each other three or four years ago. He had been in sports management for some time and had been responsible for promoting sports stars' affairs such as Gordon Banks, Chris Lewis and Andy Peake of Leicester City, to name but a few. During the 80s Barry Hearne was managing me, so John had never approached me with an offer. When we bumped into each other again, I was nearing the end of my snooker-playing career but John agreed to take me on as a client and manage my various sources of revenue. I came to John as someone with a fair amount of baggage, notably my tax problems, my gambling and subsequent bankruptcy. I told him that I had finished with betting which, in my terms, I had. I was not on the chase at this particular point of my life, but my losses were accumulating. Things were still under control but then everything changed in the early days of 2002.

I'd been able to make a reasonable living up to this point but then I realised my tax returns were in a terrible mess and that I owed a lot of money to the Inland Revenue as well as to the bookmakers. I was becoming so desperate that I resorted to using a money-lender to borrow £25,000. My credit rating with the big firms was so low that this was the only avenue left open to me.

I was living with Jill and her two children and I thought I was able to hide my mess away from them and function in a more-or-less normal way at home. They must have realised that I was under some pressure, as I was often downstairs watching television until three or four in the morning, worrying about what I was going to do the next day. Bills were coming in which I just couldn't pay and there was little work around. I had lost my place on the tour and exhibition work was becoming harder and harder to find. Commentating was bringing in some money but it was not a constant stream of cash and there were long gaps between televised tournaments. In short, I was in big trouble.

When I realised this unavoidable truth, I moved once more into that compulsive stage of gambling, the chase. When you reach this stage, you feel fated to lose and cannot see yourself ever winning again. You see your horses get boxed in, fall over, unseat their rider and so on. The £25,000 I borrowed from the money-lender relieved the strain straightaway. I was confident that I was going to win some dough again but this phase passed very quickly as hard reality bit. Ten thousand pounds went immediately to someone I owed, leaving me with a fairly small cushion to play with. I was having to pay the money lender £400 per week in interest alone, which prevented me from going for the really big bet to settle things once and for all.

Being on the chase meant it was increasingly hard to conceal my problems at home. My mood swings were all too obvious to Jill and her children. The kids would come home from school and find Mr Grumpy on the phone or watching Ceefax for the racing results. I was not the easiest person to live with. Sometimes, I would be ecstatic but too often I'd be a bad-tempered, old sod sitting in front of the telly absorbed in a world of my own. I was still borrowing money from friends in an effort to pay off the debt with the money-lender as the pressure built. Eventually, I managed to get the £25,000 paid off but in the process I had had to pay out £42,000. The financial cost was considerable and the whole episode had caused so much pain, upset and worry to people around me.

Paying off the money-lender did not mean I had turned any corner. I was in deep trouble and my self-esteem was plummeting. My failure to stay on the snooker tour was a constant niggle and did nothing to lift me out of my depression. My two rocks at this awful time were my mother and Jill. Their support was amazing in what was a very difficult time for them both, watching helplessly as my money drained away. I was making promises to them about my gambling but I carried on deceiving them as I groped for a way out of my mess.

I sought outside help at this awful time. I realised that I was suffering from depression and told the doctor I felt so low that I wanted to top myself. I started taking Prozac and managed to steer clear of suicide, though my feelings of inadequacy pushed me to the brink once or twice.

John Hayes was brilliant during these difficult years and spent hours and hours of his time making phone calls, arranging dates, organising functions and a million other things. He has spared no effort in trying to get me back on track and has worked miracles in solving some of my financial problems. I had a major problem with the Inland Revenue and, at one stage, owed £160,000 and was in danger of losing my house and being declared bankrupt yet again. Part of this huge debt – £40,000 in fact – was made up of penalties incurred over the years before I came under John's wing. I had always had such a lax attitude to tax affairs, banking on a big betting win or that I was going to earn a lot more on the snooker circuit. The tax people tend to leave you alone until your debts with them reach enormous proportions. Then they cling to you like a leech.

John came up with the idea of organising a series of events to form what was basically my testimonial year. Together, we approached Leicestershire's leading businessmen and professional people, asking them to contribute as members of my testimonial year committee. The committee was made up of Warwick Spearing and Charles Hamilton, solicitors; taxation expert, Bob Appleby; financial specialist Ian Mattioli and entrepreneurs, Matthew Hayes, Dominic Gomersall, Simon Colebeck, Kevin Ingram, Richard Hayes, Richard Grudgings and John Tyrrel. The committee was completed with British amateur golf legend, Gary Wolstenholme.

The efforts of these men ensured that the year was a great success, and I owe them all a great deal of thanks for their support and loyalty through a very trying time. To this day they all remain good personal friends and I look back on the year and what we achieved with pride. However, at the time when I was attending the committee meetings, I was not fully engaged in what was being discussed. I would put in my sixpenn'orth, but I was simply going through the motions, being in the blackest of depressions.

My testimonial year was organised in little over a month due to my pressing financial difficulties, a record, I'm sure, for this types of venture. Then, just as I began to see a light at the end of the tunnel, the Inland Revenue started their final proceedings to reclaim the amount I owed them, or force me into bankruptcy. There seemed to be no way out and I was going to be made bankrupt two weeks before the first event, ending the year before it had even begun. The thought of losing everything was very difficult to cope with … a second time.

Within two weeks there was a great deal of interest and support for the first event. Following this, we planned a succession of events throughout the year, and with this John managed to clinch a last

I'm finding a new life as an after-dinner speaker, and am photographed here enjoying a joke with Tommy Docherty, Gary and Devon Malcolm.

minute deal with the Inland Revenue, in which I was to pay back the tax bill at the rate of £10,000 per month. It would be a struggle, but the committee were very positive and we continued with the year.

The first event was held in January 2002 at Leicester City's old Filbert Street stadium, an ideal location for a life-long City fan. We managed to attract a star-studded line-up featuring Rick Wakeman, Jasper Carrott, Roger DeCourcey and Renato, the like of which Leicester had rarely seen for such an event and we sold out in no time.

The support I received from my committee, guests and celebrity friends was incredible, and kept me going through the darkest of times. An extra special thankyou must go to Jasper Carrott, whose mother was very unwell and was taken to hospital on the night of the event. After a brilliant 45-minute set, he made his apologies and headed straight back to be with his mother.

The evening was a great success and we set about planning others like it to meet our promise to the Inland Revenue. The next event was held at the prestigious Quorn Hotel in Leicestershire. Dennis Taylor lent his support, along with one of the funniest men of the circuit, Micky Gunn. Amongst the many local events were those organised by the Leicester Tigers Rugby Club, through their chairman, Peter Tom. These included articles in match programmes, sales promotions and a half-time welcome on to the pitch. Sharing a field with 20-stone giants like Martin Johnson and Co, served to cement my preference for the genteel green baize.

However, all the support and glamour of my testimonial year still could not shake off the financial pressure I was under, and depression was still very much a part of my everyday life, and disaster never very far away.

We were planning a huge event at the prestigious Grosvenor House Hotel in London for the middle of the year. Being crucial to the success of the whole year, a great deal of attention was being focused on every detail. A large headline act was needed to attract the thousand or so guests we had planned and we tried to book Tom Jones. For a while it seemed as if he might be able to squeeze us into his busy diary, but, just as we were about to finalise the arrangement, a large contract in Monte Carlo came up, and that was that.

We had raised quite a bit from four or five successful events, then came a two-month period when we just couldn't pay the taxmen anything. The situation looked dire and my depression deepened, leading me to commit one of those selfish acts which I will feel ashamed about forever: I broke my promise to John and started to gamble again. There seemed to be no other way out, and yet I knew that not only was I letting John down, but also my wife and mother.

I'd tried Prozac tablets in the past and they'd given me some respite. This time my depression seemed so much more intense. I can remember going into the bedroom and sitting on the edge of our bed and staring at the bottles of pills I'd brought in from the medicine cabinet. It was such a cowardly, despicable thing I was considering. Why choose my own home? Why leave it for my wife to be the first to discover me? What a complete shit ...

There were 30 sleeping tablets in the containers left over from times when I'd been unable to sleep. I gazed at them again and realised how lonely I felt sitting there in an empty house. Jill was out at a lecture, the kids were at school and there was little chance of being discovered. I wrote out a note and then started to gulp down the tablets three at a time until they were all gone. I remember falling back on the pillow closing my eyes and waiting for sleep. I didn't realise how exhausted I was after all those days of worry and depression and soon I was asleep.

I'm not sure about the exact details of what happened next. Apparently, Jill's son, James, came home and saw me lying on the bed asleep but thought nothing of it. When his mum arrived back from Leicester, she realised straightaway what was going on and rang for an ambulance and then had the harrowing task of following in her car as the ambulance crew worked on me all the way to the hospital.

I was lucky and not for the first time in my life. I'd been found in time and woke up in a hospital bed. I felt so miserable, not because I'd survived but because my bed was surrounded by a group of distraught people I had let down. My brothers were both there, along with Jill, Mum and John, the very people to whom I'd already caused so much pain.

It's very difficult writing about all this, but I felt that I had to include it, partly by way of apology and partly as a warning to those on the edge of major betting problems. Gambling is a real illness. It is so addictive and destructive in its effects on the gambler, but what makes it so powerful as a social disease, is the appalling effect it has on family and friends. The lying, the breaking of trust are too high a price to for those short moments of ecstasy.

chapter twelve
RECOVERY

I have managed to pull myself back from the brink and, thanks to John, I have been able to clear my tax arrears. It has been a long slow road with so many functions, dinners and golf days supported by good friends including Jasper Carrott, Rick Wakeman, Jimmy Tarbuck, Nigel Mansell and Ian Botham, as well as my snooker pals like Dennis Taylor. Gary was on the committee and, typically, he threw a lot of his support my way.

The strategy has taken a long time to work but my life has been put back on a more even keel with my gambling firmly in check. Now I work for John in his corporate hospitality and sports promotions business, Champions UK. He manages all my affairs now and, with the contacts I have built up over the years, I have been able to pay back something towards the debt I owe him as a partner and, more importantly, as a friend.

I have built up a whole host of contacts through my long career in the game. I have a lot of friends in snooker, people I have known for over a quarter of a century as we've come through the ranks together. More recently, I have made a lot of friends in the world of showbiz and other sports through my work as an after-dinner speaker and playing on golf celebrity days. Slowly, my finances are getting straight, not easy when you are responsible for two families and two houses.

Jill and I married in January 2003 after living together for eight years and this sort of commitment has made me promise not to get into the same mess again. I had avoided the subject of marriage for so many years, using that well worn line about the contract being just a piece of paper with very little meaning. I am amazed at the effect it has had on me in the months since I made the commitment to Jill. It has helped me so much in the recovery process, giving me a depth of stability that I haven't experienced before in my life. I know it sounds very clichéd, but Jill has been a rock in my life and she has helped me through these last difficult years in a way few other people could. She understands the depressive condition I suffer from and is so good at coping with me and taking me through my dark times. I can deal with the condition far better now, even in January and February when the weather is so dreary and work not easy to find. I am not saying that I am cured but I have strategies and the support to help me cope.

There are still financial strains, though nothing like those dark days of bankruptcy and mountainous tax arrears. I am still paying my first wife the alimony that was set in the late 80s and have still got a huge mortgage millstone around my neck. Originally, the payments were only £800 per month but when my gambling debts started to bite, I renegotiated the repayment so that now £1,700 is leaving my bank account every month. Jill's first husband has to contribute to the maintenance of my two step-children but basically I need £1,000 a week just to keep my head above water.

The temptation to gamble is still there but the memory of letting people down is a strong one. I haven't been inside a betting shop for years and I have been barred by Tattersalls from attending race meetings because of past indiscretions, so another source of temptation has been removed. I am not saying that I will never gamble again. I may have as much as £200 in my pocket at any one time but I am under no illusions that this amount could fund a series of big wins. It certainly couldn't change my life and so I'm not tempted to go back to my old ways. I will still have a flutter if I am in a casino with friends but my betting is well under control. I still do the Lottery every Wednesday and Saturday, so I suppose, deep down, I am still looking for that big win, but I think that feeling is just the vestiges of my craving for excitement.

I mustn't complain: I have too much to be grateful for. My days as a really high earner are over, though I am still optimistic about the future. The days of expensive holidays and having help in the home are gone but Jill and I do enjoy a very pleasant life. She is studying for an Honours degree, in Leicester, but her commitments enable her to come with me to about a third of my golfing and commentating dates. We stay in good hotels and meet up with people who are regulars on the circuit. Admittedly, we must have seen some cabaret acts so many times that we are now word perfect in most of the jokes and routines. But this is my job now and I am very fortunate to be able to live such a luxurious life style. The summer always used to be a killer for me when I was at the top because it was the closed season with no work for 16 weeks. There was always a lot of time to fill and, with my gambling problem, it was so tempting to while away those days at the races or betting on something else. Nowadays, the summer is a busy time for me as I am often away playing golf in a celebrity tournament somewhere.

The real godsend for me in this autumn of my career, however, has been the development of corporate hospitality and its link up with sport. Companies have been using sport to reward employees and market their products. I have been able to break into this circuit, not through my prowess on the snooker table, but bizarrely (you might think) through my golf skills. I am a reasonable player now, with eight years of fairly regular playing behind me. I have actually been playing since I was in my teens but I only took the game up seriously when I was advised by the doctor to play again after I had had a little bit of a twinge in the ticker. My handicap is 14 and I can go round most golf courses scoring in the mid-80s and hitting a few decent shots per round.

I first hit the celebrity golf circuit through a Benson and Hedges invitational event. I have always had the reputation as a bit of a character and a good chatterer but, basically, I realise I was just lucky to be in the right place at the right time. B & H had used Cliff and Dennis and, as I had been involved with them for a long time through various sponsored events, I suppose it was inevitable that they would get round to me eventually.

The basis of the corporate hospitality circuit is that firms will pay celebrities, sporting and otherwise, to play a round of golf with their clients and then attend lunches, dinners and cabarets with them. I have still got a fairly high profile through my commentating work and through my lingering reputation as a top player of yesteryear. Most of the guys I play will remember me from those days and the distinctive hairstyle and the moustache are excellent memory joggers.

I am employed these days not just to play golf but also to chat and dazzle people with my wit. Usually, it's a really enjoyable way to spend a day or two, playing on championship golf courses where the green fees are well in excess of £100. It can be very nerve wracking to play as a 14-handicapper on a golf course in front of a gallery and I can still remember my nervousness when I stepped out on the first tee for my debut on the celebrity circuit. It is so easy to slice or hook and, even though we play off the yellow tees while the pro golfers play off the whites, we are often faced with a crowd of 20 or more spectators forming an avenue in front of us.

I did have one appalling moment on the Mere course in Cheshire when I was playing in the Howard Keel Classic. I had laid up just in front of a water hazard with a seven iron before hitting a sand wedge to the green. There was a gallery of about 200 people waiting for my shot and I thinned it. I shouted a warning but there was no chance of a little girl getting out of the way in time. Her head swelled up immediately as she lay on the ground. She was rushed off to hospital and I was left in a complete mess. I couldn't carry on so I just walked off the course and drove over to see her. Fortunately she was alright and was back watching the next day, but the whole incident had really scared me. It is a hazard of the job and, touch wood, nothing like it has happened since.

It is difficult to turn down requests from charities and fundraisers like the Variety Club, but the hotel life, with days away from home, can be boring. I accept it now as a really important contributor to my livelihood. In the last two years I have come to appreciate the value of these celebrity days, as I reckon I now generate at least 40 per cent of my work through the contacts I make while playing golf. I still get the chance to play golf away from the circuit, though there does seem to be less and less time these days. I am still a member at Kilworth Springs but I probably only manage six rounds a year. I do a couple of dinners for the owners, Roger and Ann Vickery, and I put on an annual charity event at the club for Age Concern with Gary Wolstenholme, the pro.

There are so many perks that go with this job. I get the chance to hear and see some of the country's best entertainers at the evening functions and eat some really good food. Occasionally, I have been invited back to the homes of some of the wonderful people I have met. It's interesting to go to beautiful places, though I often reflect on the time when I had a luxury house and an extravagant life style.

After-dinner speaking is a real growth area for other snooker pros. Dennis, Steve, JP and John Virgo have all made it on to the circuit. Three or four years ago, the after-dinner speakers were mainly drawn from football and cricket but there is now a market for a whole variety of sports personalities. I have gradually built up my patter over the years and I now stand up and give about 40 minutes of bollocks. Occasionally, I am able to do a snooker exhibition and then a trick shot routine but this sort of venue is becoming harder and harder to find.

There is a limit in any area of the country to the number of occasions when I could deliver my routine. I know that Jack Charlton has been doing the same stuff for years at four grand a time, but he's an exception. I'd love to be able to do it two or three times a week but I have not reached the top of the circuit and to speak so often would probably mean the kiss of death through over exposure. I am able to vary the routine by taking questions from the floor after I have done my repertoire of jokes and reminiscences. I have been able to steer clear of blue jokes though I can't resist the odd innuendo, especially with a nickname like Big Willie. I have also avoided the trap of slagging people off. I know Tommy Smith has made a career out of his hatred of Emlyn Hughes but I would find it hard to tell tales out of school about my fellow pros.

This new career of mine is obviously the way forward, as I can now earn far more from speaking than I can from playing. I have just managed to get a string of dates from David Duckham, the old England Rugby Union winger. He is now in the hospitality industry and, amongst other things, organises dinners at sporting clubs. These dinners are black tie affairs and usually finish with a comedian like Max Boyce or Stan Boardman. There are a number of entertainers who are no longer on television much these days but are, nevertheless, making a lucrative living on the dinner circuit.

I am generating work more and more work as my reputation spreads. There are lots of corporate hospitality sites on the internet and it has been easy to circulate my brochure around a huge market. It's a slow process but I am very hopeful at last after a really dark period in my life. I have lost the motivation to base my life on snooker, partly because my skills are in decline but mainly because the openings in exhibition work and seniors tournaments are just not there. I still love the game and miss the thrill of playing and winning. Although I enjoy talking about it with my peers and love the excitement of commentating at big tournaments, nothing compares with the highs you go through when you are a competitor playing at the top of your game.

Surrounded by the people who mean the most to me, Jill, my mother, and my children.

chapter thirteen
EPILOGUE

The last two or three years have brought a new set of problems, as I have had to come to terms with the realisation that I am no longer a top snooker professional. My pride was hurt when I was passed over as a wildcard for tournaments and had to go through the laborious process of qualification, after a career when I had enjoyed automatic invitations to all the major tournaments.

I admit some jealousy towards the likes of Ken Doherty, Stephen Hendry and Mark Williams and wish that I was younger and fit enough to take them on. I'll never get back to my old level: I accept that now. However, during my downward spiral in the 90s, it became difficult to accept that fact. Every now and then, there would be another knock to my ego as my standing in the game gradually ebbed away. Occasionally, resentment crept in when I felt that the goal posts were being moved. I had been given a wild card to play in the Liverpool Victoria tournament. The agreement was to run for three years but, in the final year, I was given the push by the sponsors after they'd been forced over a barrel by Ian Doyle. He wanted one of his players, Alain Robidoux, to play and threatened to pull his trump card, Stephen Hendry, out of the tournament, if he didn't get his way. I went berserk. My pride had been hurt and, although I was given some compensation, I was resentful. I'd been stitched up.

I could tell that the end was coming in the 1998/99 season when I failed to make it to the main tour. I missed out on wild card entries to the Embassy World Championship and other tournaments and that really hit home. I had to come to terms with the fact that I wasn't Willie Thorne the snooker player anymore, that the high earnings and all the trappings that go with fame and fortune were no longer mine and that I would have to diversify to keep up a reasonable life style.

It took me a long time to come to terms with the decline that inevitably affects all sportsmen. I still had a lot of faith in my own ability but the results I was achieving didn't really bear this out. Slowly, my skill drained away from me as, bit by bit, my hand-eye co-ordination deteriorated. My eyes progressively started to lie to me. I was reaching the stage where I would hit the ball in what would look like the perfect spot and I'd be amazed when it would rattle round the jaws of the pocket without sinking. In my prime, when hit correctly, I knew the ball would be sunk without even watching it drop.

I still feel that, even in the modern game, I can score heavily around the black spot but, as soon as I'm called to make a long pot, my confidence evaporates. I just don't have the eyesight and co-ordination to take on these crucial shots. I found, as time went by, that I was losing to younger players who, although they were beating me fair and square, were not up to the standard I'd reached in my heyday.

As I slipped down the rankings, I became increasingly depressed about my game. Uncharacteristically, I got involved with the occasional dispute as I became more and more desperate to stay on the professional tour. I once played Feargal O'Brien in a qualifier at the Norbreck Castle in Blackpool. If I'd lost to him, I would have had to win the next two matches to stay on the tour. I managed to snooker him and put myself into a commanding position to win the frame. He played a shot that couldn't possibly target the ball and missed by a foot. Unbelievably, the referee replaced the ball and declared that it was a good attempt. My concentration disappeared as my anger rose and, sure enough, I lost the frame. It was the fifth frame and I would have gone 3-2 ahead but now my concentration was shattered as the incident preyed on me. Now I had the hump. The toys came out of the pram as I sulked my way to defeat, looking for excuses. As everybody in the game knows, I have a million excuses – I had a cold, I tripped over hair, etc, etc. The lads will all tell you that under my bed I've got a wooden box labelled Virgin Excuses, full of immunities from blame and excuses that haven't been told yet.

What made the whole Feargal O'Brien episode even more galling was the admission I overheard afterwards from Feargal when he was chatting to his mates on the phone. He was delighted to have got the scalp of Willie Thorne – now there's a thought! However, when I heard him telling his mates that the ref's decision had suited him, I wanted to chin him. He thought he would get away with the shot and trick the referee into what I still think was a very dodgy decision. He hadn't done anything wrong but he had acted outside the spirit of the game. Characteristically, this match played on my mind for ages and it was a year before I spoke to him again.

A match against Andy Hicks, in the late 80s, saw the same thing happen to me when I was leading by 50 in the last frame of the evening session. We were in the last 16 of the World Championships at the Crucible and I was trailing 9-6. This was a really important match for me to win, as I was in danger of slipping out of the top rankings and of losing out on all the invitations and exhibition work that came with such a position. There was a red over the top pocket and we were playing cautiously, just tip-tapping our way around the pack in fear of dislodging a ball to leave an easy opening. The referee ruled that we could have three shots each before he would make me play another type of shot. Sure enough, when we had finished our trio of shots, I was forced to play for a ridiculous plant. I missed it and even though I'd been 40 ahead, my confidence just drained away and I lost the frame, ending the evening 10-6 down and furious. Needless to say, the next day dawned with me reaching for the wooden box under the bed ...

At the very end of my career, I was playing Dominic Dale at Telford in a qualifier. It was crucial for me to win the match and I started quite well and had a 3-2 lead when referee, John Williams, made me replay a shot. I fell to pieces, lost the session 6-2 and eventually the match 10-6. I over-reacted. I was seething and went berserk in the locker room afterwards. Williams, in his interview afterwards, said that he thought I'd be a good player if I didn't do so much huffing and puffing.

On its own, that decline would be hard to take, as it is for every sports person, when facing the reality that the skills which have taken him to the top of the sporting tree are now in terminal decline. The process of accepting the obvious is not a simple one because the fall is not steady, nor is it gradual. There are spells when results start to improve but this merely postpones the inevitable.

Running parallel with the decline in the sporting arena is the effect it has on one's fame and celebrity. Most people who have been in the public eye for some period of their life will enjoy the perks of fame. It is really nice 90 per cent of the time to be in a public place and for someone to approach you for a quick chat and an autograph. There are some idiots out there who might want to be unpleasant and score points off you but I can look back on so many instances when people have been genuinely kind and generous to me, both in their comments and their hospitality.

In many ways I have been lucky in these last few years that I have still been able to enjoy recognition on the street, in restaurants or wherever. The 'tache and the haircut obviously help people who have been following snooker for years to recognise me without going through the agony of, "It's 'im, isn't it?" My television work has helped to keep up a certain level of celebrity and I am well aware of the need for me to stay in the public spotlight from a purely financial point of view.

Snooker provided me with a very comfortable living when I was at the top and I should really be enjoying the fruits of my success for the rest of my life but I have probably squandered more than one and a half million pounds on gambling. I have been an absolute plonker to let it happen, not just once, but in two separate drawn-out periods.

My action gambling was exciting and to some extent it came with the territory. I can look back on some great experiences on the racecourse or in the betting shop but I know I must not wallow in these reminiscences. Gambling has cost me dear. It helped to break up a marriage and destroy another long term relationship and it separated me from my children as they were growing up.

My mother and my wife, Jill, have seen me at my lowest ebb. Jill, in particular, has had to deal with my mood swings and my descent into depression but has always stood by me. The support and love they have given me has been totally unconditional and, in their different ways, they have pulled me back from the dire straits I found myself in at the end of 2002.

I am Willie Thorne – Mr Maximum – and a man with the optimism to face the future and a determination never again to allow gambling to get its pernicious hold on me. I still have my box of excuses but I am saving up for a padlock.

Postscript
THE MODERN GAME

I've been fortunate over the last decade to get a chance to commentate. I was first asked by Whispering Ted Lowe to commentate on *Junior Pot Black*. There was a link between me as the youngest ever contestant in the tournament in the 1970s but Ted never told me why he'd given me the chance. I respected him as a commentator and as a really nice man but as we were not especially close friends, nobody could really accuse me of getting into commentating through some networking.

I quite enjoyed that first experience as the 'Colour' commentator. It was my role to add a few remarks to the lead commentator's general description of the game. With my knowledge of shot making, I was able to point to the type of technique the player was about to use in playing the next shot, which ball would be next and so on. I remember doing a commentary on Stephen Hendry, who was making his first appearance on *Junior Pot Black*. I went a bit over the top in my evaluation of the young Scot's talent and actually criticised little Stephen. I remember saying that I thought he was too small to do well and that he would have to change his action. He was finding some shots difficult to reach and so his contact with the ball was somewhat sideways. By stretching and reaching across the table, it was difficult for Stephen to play smoothly through the ball. I remember Alan Hansen making a wild statement about the youthfulness of the Manchester United side in the late 90s, dismissing their chances of winning titles by saying, "You never win anything with kids." He's been teased about it ever since, just as Stephen ribs me about my remarks whenever he sees me.

This venture into commentating came when I was still a top 16 player and it was something I didn't throw myself into. I did the occasional job for the BBC, but I got a bit fed up with the uncertainty of knowing whether and when they would next employ me. At the time, I didn't see it as a long-term prospect as I was busy with my career playing in tournaments and exhibitions and, basically, I didn't really have the time to devote to a second career in the media.

However, as my snooker career has waned, commentating has become an increasingly important part of my life. I am still employed by all three channels as a freelance commentator, unlike John Virgo and Dennis Taylor who are both contracted to the BBC. I have not received any formal training and basically the producers allow me to get on with the job. They remind me from time to time of the fault that I am very aware of – I talk too much.

I can't resist making comments before a shot is played. Let's face it, any commentator can make a remark after a player has had his turn at the table. As I was a really good break-builder, I find this side of the game the most compelling one to analyse. Hendry and O'Sullivan would both be excellent commentators, as this ability to score heavily in a single visit to the table is where both of them are way ahead of their peers. I receive many letters about my commentating style, some of them having the obvious dig – "Well if you know so much, how come you're not still playing?"

Other people have been more complimentary. I received 2,000 letters one year for talking through the painstaking build-up of a 147 break on television. People said they were grateful for the information as the break developed, especially as I try to think two or three shots ahead. This was the way I played for my maximums and it is the only situation where a player should be thinking that far ahead in a frame. I get a genuine buzz as I talk through a maximum break. It's one of those rare situations in sport where everybody, crowd, commentators, even the opponent, is behind the guy who has tied the frame up and is working towards the maximum. When the commentator screams over the applause of the audience at the end of a 147 break, it is completely heartfelt and in no way contrived.

I have had no voice training for the job but I've been told I've got a clear voice and that I'm a good speaker. I've never really found it difficult speaking at dinners or acting as an MC. I suppose it's a skill that develops over the years as you are forced to face the Press, make acceptance speeches, or chat away to audiences at exhibitions. What surprises some people is the tone of my voice when I'm commentating, especially if they've heard me speak to an audience in public. I have a naturally deep, loud voice yet, when I commentate, my voice is a lot lighter. Perhaps I've just picked up the virus from Whispering Ted.

Not every snooker player is able to commentate, even though they know the game inside out. Eddie Charlton, Ray Reardon and Alex Higgins were all given trials for television but didn't come up to scratch in explaining the game in fairly simple terms. As a group, we get together quite a lot and chat about the game. This is inevitable since we are usually staying in the same hotel for a week while a tournament progresses. We rarely argue for hours about a game, as people would do after a game of football. I think we appreciate the fact that all good snooker players have their own ways of looking at a match, or a frame, and they're all equally valid interpretations. I respect the views of Parrott, Virgo, Davis and Taylor when commentating. They have all played at the highest level and can all present their own view on why a frame was lost or which shot selection would have been better at a certain point in the game. I think we all have the expertise to show the layman the validity of our comments and I think this adds to the enjoyment that most people get from watching a game of snooker.

The new regime at the BBC has favoured the employment of ex-sports stars as commentators. We're encouraged to chat about other things, like the meal the night before, family, the letters we've had from viewers. This has been a deliberate policy by the BBC to make the game more appealing to a younger generation. I suppose the template for this is Peter Allis' golf commentaries, which he manages to make funny in an effortless way. When you have a huge viewing slot to fill, it's vital to break up the match, especially if it's a slow, tactical one. You don't want to spend two and a half hours just talking about tactics, though I must admit I get my fair share of letters telling me that I talk too much and should just shut up, cut out the waffle and stick to match analysis.

Basically, the level of snooker commentary is high. A football match, probably because of the speed of the game, tends to be very descriptive while the match is in progress. We'll be told that x passes to y and shoots. There is a tendency for commentators to tell us what's happening to the ball and not to tell the viewer what is developing in other parts of the pitch. The post-match analysis is improving, though the depth is dependent on the time allowed by the producer at the end of a game. In contrast, the slow nature of the game of snooker allows the commentator to make comments about the quality of a shot, or whether the cue ball has been moved into position for the build up of a break.

During the World Championships viewing figures are still astronomical. We still attract two and a half million in an afternoon on BBC2 at a time when most stations would be grateful for a fifth of that number. Obviously, we will never achieve the huge figures of the 1980s when I won the Mercantile with an audience of 12 million and Dennis Taylor's Embassy World Championship victory over Steve Davis attracted 18 million. Satellite television and the explosion of choice means we will never again reach that size of audience but we still have a very loyal support base. The age profile of our audience is a cause for worry, as the overwhelming majority fall into the 40-80 age category, most of whom were hooked on snooker in the boom days of the 1980s. It is far more difficult today to attract sponsorship to the game when our fan base lies outside the crucial 19-35 age group; the group that spends the most money and is the main target for the advertising companies.

There has also been a relaxation of the dress code to broaden the game's appeal. I have always been very conservative about this issue and I was sad to see the days of the bow tie and the suit put to an end by the BBC. Alex Higgins had been given permission years ago to dispense with the bow tie when it started to irritate his throat. He just loved ripping it off and listening to the applause from the crowd. Sky too, have experimented with various ways of tweaking the image and presentation of the game. The idea of getting one player to dress in red with his opponent in blue has been tried, although I don't think it will be repeated.

I cannot forecast the way my commentating career will go. I have graduated to lead commentator, though we all take turns in doing that job. The hardest job, by far, is the live hosting of a snooker tournament, which involves working with an autocue. On the face of it, this would seem to be an absolute doddle, reading a script that scrolls in front of you below the camera. In truth, I find it far from easy and I'm still slightly in awe of the way presenters like Hazel Irvine and Gary Lineker have perfected the technique. When Gary first started, I must admit I didn't think he'd make it as a commentator. He was so wooden and nothing like the relaxed, witty bloke I knew. Now he's developed into a professional who's as good as Desmond Lynam. He seems to get better and better as he takes on more and more demanding jobs. He is obviously highly thought of at the BBC as he's been given crucial anchor jobs in flagship programmes such as BBC Sports Personality Of The Year. He is now so relaxed in front of the camera that he can cope with almost any eventuality – even when the autocue jams or breaks down completely. He's a role model for any of the ex-sports stars the BBC seem keen to use nowadays.

The position of anchorman on any sports programme is a difficult one to fill but we've been lucky in snooker to have had a series of really good presenters. David Vine set the standard in the 70s and 80s followed by Dougie Donnelly, who was a real snooker enthusiast. Now Hazel Irvine has taken over and, after a shaky start, has made massive strides. She is very confident in front of the cameras and now has a much bigger armoury of facts and an impressive appreciation of the finer points of the game. Hazel has really worked at it and is now one of the best all-round sports presenters on television.

Besides the commentating, I knew I could still earn money on the exhibition circuit. I could still trade on my name and reputation and would be able to put on exhibitions with John Virgo and Dennis Taylor. Sometimes we would play big leisure centres with as many as 1500 in the audience, but we would be on the undercard to the main attractions: Jimmy White, Stephen Hendry or Ronnie O'Sullivan.

In the last couple of years, the exhibition circuit has declined rapidly, although Jimmy is still in demand. John accompanies him as he's built up a following through his television work with Jim Davidson on *Big Break* as the guy with a whole host of trick shots up his sleeve and a great line in patter and cruel impressions of other snooker players. These two are probably the busiest on the exhibition circuit and, in the quiet times between tournaments, they may do a couple a week for two grand a time. Ronnie O'Sullivan is a busy guy as well but Steve Davis and Stephen Hendry now are very choosy. They charge as much as £4,000 an appearance but there are few places that can raise that amount through the box office.

Nowadays, the exhibition circuit has virtually dried up for me. I still get the occasional invitation but I am finding it increasingly difficult to stay on top of my game. It's becoming harder and harder for me to motivate myself to do some serious practice when, at the end of it, I'll be picking up less than £1,000 for an evening. To most people, that would appear to be a decent fee but when you think of the hours of practice you need to put in before an exhibition and the time and money spent travelling to a venue, the rate becomes less attractive. It seems strange for me to say this about snooker, the game I have loved playing for so long, but the simple truth is that I don't enjoy practising any more. It takes me so long each time I approach an exhibition match to get my timing back. My cueing arm needs attention because I am finding that I am over-hitting and under-hitting too many balls. My biggest weakness is my inability to pot long shots and embarrassingly missing them by miles. I am sure that if there were more exhibitions around, say one a week, I'd be more motivated and I would practise harder.

The resurgence of an exhibition circuit does seem a bit of a long shot at the moment, as does the development of a Seniors Tour. On the face of it, with so many of the top 16 in their early 30s or younger, you would think there would be a market for the golden oldies to build on the nostalgia amongst snooker's core audience and develop a tour. Steve Davis, Jimmy White and John Parrott are all over 40 and they're all trying their utmost to stay at the top. At present they see their immediate future in the snooker tour but there may come a time when they will lend their considerable kudos to the establishment of a Seniors Tour.

There is certainly the desire amongst the older players from the boom years to develop something. I know that Tony Knowles, Mike Hallett, Joe Johnson and Ray Reardon are interested, as are the Canadians, Thorburn, Stevens and Wych. The simple fact is that these overseas players cannot afford to break back into the old tour. It would cost them £20,000 on air fares and hotels just to come over and work their way through the qualifying rounds. It always seems

My last professional victory in the World Seniors Masters Tournament in 2000.

unfair that an iconic World Champion like Cliff Thorburn is not given a wild card. It's a shame that snooker doesn't follow the example of the golf majors and bring back the former World Champions and allow them to compete. I know I am biased but I think we need to keep the modern game's links with its past and give audiences the chance to see veterans play again. I feel confident that the reaction amongst spectators would be the same as when Jack Nicklaus and Tom Watson played in the tournaments they won two decades ago. A similar approach could so easily be used in our game.

There has been one attempt so far to launch the seniors concept. In 2000, Sky televised the first World Seniors Masters Tournament over the Christmas period. This is probably the worst time of year to launch this type of tournament as there is so much competition for television audiences. They revived the old *Pot Black* formula of single frame matches and tried to give it a twist by employing Mark King, a younger player, as the commentator. I think the tournament was crying out for someone that people would associate with the 80s and the players who were taking part. Ted Lowe was the obvious candidate.

I felt sorry for Peter Bainbridge and Ralph Holt whose brainchild it was. The event on the surface had all the trappings for a successful launch. It was held in the magnificent setting of the RAC club in London. The set designer had done a great job decorating the playing area with a sumptuous display of plants and flowers and the audience was asked to dress up for the black tie event. The trophy was a very expensive, gold £50,000 claret jug, similar to the one presented to the Open Golf Champion. There was a modest £10,000 first prize to go with the kudos of the title.

The audience comprised only about 80, all in dinner jackets. There was an expensive lunch before the afternoon session and dinner was provided before the players went out for the final frames in the evening. As much as £50,000 would have been spent on hire charges for the club and all the other back up elements that go hand in hand with a televised event. In total, there was probably a quarter of a million pounds invested in the event. The saying goes that you have to speculate to accumulate and Peter Bainbridge did this in bucketfuls.

I practised hard and managed to win the inaugural event which was played over a single frame. I had played Joe Johnson in the first round before defeating the Silver Fox. Rex Williams was next before I defeated Cliff in the final. If I am honest, the snooker was crap. I managed a break of 60 in the final but, generally, the standard was so poor it would have been difficult to sell it around the country.

That turned out to be the only time the tournament was staged. The formula just hadn't worked and the list of potential sponsors dried up. The first event had relied on television money but Sky were reluctant to commit themselves again and without money, it was a catch-22 situation. The senior players would only turn up if they were guaranteed appearance money and, without the competitors, no meaningful tournament could take place and so no television money would come in.

Snooker must really try to reinvent itself and bring more variety to the structure and format of tournaments. Who knows, the Seniors may be revived but at least winning the trophy, which is now in a display case at the RAC, entitles me to call myself the undefeated reigning World Seniors Masters Champion.

I have done a pilot programme with Cliff Thorburn that might take off. The concept is that the table is a smaller 9ft by 5ft and the game is played with just eleven reds. The game is called Diamond Snooker and has the advantage for me of there being no long shots in a frame. We played against a couple of lady players. It was a good game with the highlight being the maximum scored by Cliff the Grinder. It is far easier to move the balls around and it makes for an attractive game. The pilot has been sent off to all the channels and we are just waiting with fingers crossed for it to be properly promoted.

Changes to the game

I have been asked many times about how I rate my fellow professionals and on the changes in snooker over the years. Since I have become more involved in commentating, I have had the opportunity to reflect on these matters. Being in the commentary box focuses the mind. You start to think more and more deeply about the game. The temptation for ex-players of any game is to bemoan the state of the modern game. There is a tendency amongst a lot of soccer players, in particular, to criticise the modern player, partly through jealousy. It is not surprising that they feel envious when they look at the salaries earned by the most ordinary of talents and compare them with the amounts they got out of the game, although some ex-players sometimes have a very inflated opinion of their own ability, making them feel they have the right to be condescending and critical.

I admire much about the modern game and its players, but it has become more and more difficult to compare today's game with the one played in the heydays of the 80s. The rules, with just a few minor exceptions, have remained the same. The cues are still more or less the same, although extensions are now a considerable improvement on the days when players used the long cues stored under the table. The fact that I still play with the cue my mother bought me in the 60s is a testament to this basic point. When somebody like Stephen Hendry smashes his cue on the way back from Thailand and then proceeds to play some of the best snooker of his life in the Brighton tournament in October 2003, you have to be in awe of him and his talent. Thankfully, I managed to show great restraint this time, as the spectre of JP sat on my shoulder whispering "Remember Motherwell 96 ..."

The really big revolution which has affected the game has come with the changes in table design. The stimulus originated in Thailand where snooker is played in a very humid environment. The tournaments there are played in large arenas with very advanced air conditioning systems. The Thais also use dehumidifiers, which produce buckets and buckets of water every day. These systems are rarely needed in Britain, as snooker is largely a winter sport.

The crucial changes in Thailand which have now been adopted worldwide are in the playing surface. The green baize used today is the thinner Thai version, which is faster than the traditional British version. It is like playing on pool cloth, with the balls travelling much faster. The introduction of table heaters has compounded the change. In Thailand, even with air conditioning and dehumidifiers, the cloth could be quite damp, making the balls run slowly. By heating the slate beneath the cloth, the playing surface is transformed and there is far more uniformity of ball speed across the snooker world. I always thought when I played at the Crucible or the Guild Hall, in Preston, that conditions were perfect before the changes in table technology. The standard of play was fantastic and the strategies employed by players far more varied than is the case today.

Recently, it has been noticeable with the aid of slow motion replays, to watch balls bouncing from the surface. When a player cues down to try to stun the ball, the white will leave the bed. Even the object ball can be seen to hop in the same way. The fault lies with the cloth, which is now so fine that the game is virtually played on slate.

It has now become far easier to score heavily with one visit to the table. The balls are slightly lighter, nowadays, all produced by a single supplier, whereas, in the past, there were a number of manufacturers, including Armint and Supercrystallite. Most people would think that this would produce greater uniformity but there is still a variation from one set of balls to the next. At a tournament, you can walk from one table to another and watch the balls behaving in a totally different way. Many players can recognise the difference between cue balls from different sets. Sometimes you get what is called a 'heavy' white, at other times you will get a 'light' version. They may be the same weight but their density may be different and, as a result, they play differently. Sometimes, when you have been playing with a light ball you make what looks like a ridiculous error of judgement. I could play a cue ball to screw back a foot but its come back three feet. That's the curse of modern equipment.

The greatest difference the new table surfaces have made is that the balls are far more responsive to the impact of the cue ball. It's easier now to break up the pack. The surface is bone dry, so the balls react much more quickly. In the past, you would be lucky to get three reds coming out of the pack; nowadays, it is often possible to disturb as many as twelve. As a result, break-building becomes easier: it is not an art anymore. A lot of today's players can be seen cursing their luck if they fail to free a red from the pack when often they just seem to be hitting and hoping.

Contrary to what some people think, the pockets are still the same size in tournament play. The measuring templates used to assess the pocket size are standard for tournament as well as club play. In that respect, it is no easier to pot a ball than it was in the past, but the simple fact is that high scores are achievable far more frequently than was the case years ago. You could make a comparison with golf where the improvement in equipment has made the game more accessible to far more people. Just as in golf, however, if you took the best players from snooker clubs, and put them in tournaments, in all probability they wouldn't score a 50 break. They might impress in their own clubs by scoring centuries but, in tournament play, the pressures are totally different. What separates the top professional from the good amateur is their temperament and the consistency that comes with it.

I never had that sort of temperament, whereas Steve Davis had it by the bucketful. He had sufficient mental strength to enable him to avoid missing shots and making silly errors. I still love watching him play because he shows how much craft he's built up over the years. He's probably 21 points a frame worse than he used to be, yet he has managed to claw his way back into the top 16. He doesn't make century breaks like he used to and is probably down to a third of his quota at his height, but he is still capable of winning frames through sheer tactical skill. Steve is also buoyed immensely by the crowd nowadays. He has done brilliantly to reinvent himself by playing up to the Boring Steve Davis image from the *Spitting Image* programme. In fact, he is more popular now than when he was at the top. It is in the Englishman's nature to support the underdog and Steve as well as Jimmy White have been able to milk this trait to good effect in recent years.

You can always sense from the start how much of the crowd is on your side and it will often make a difference to your confidence, which could be crucial in deciding the game's outcome. Snooker audiences are well behaved and there is seldom an occasion where a referee has trouble controlling the crowd and maintaining the game's traditional good manners and sportsmanship.

The skill aspect of the game has undoubtedly improved in some areas of snooker. John Spencer was the first player to develop a deep screw shot in the 70s when nobody else had mastered it. Neal Foulds and Bill Werbenuik mastered it eventually and developed it further and it has now reached the point where everybody can plan this shot. So what seemed impossible 20 years ago is now commonplace. You can play 12-foot shots and screw the cue ball all the way back to the baulk cushion.

The top players have continued to push the boundaries of the game into new areas of skill. Stephen Hendry, one of snooker's all time greats, has developed a shot where he goes topside of the blue, screwing into the pink bottom, so when the cue ball hits the pink, instead of running through into the reds and settling on the black cushion, it just stops – exactly like a pool shot. None of us realised that it was a shot that could be played but Stephen invented it and has continued to improve it.

The game has also seen advances which have removed some of the elements of bad luck every player complains about. Table design has also been improved in the construction of cushions. Until recently, you could see balls coming off cushions at a ridiculous speed but now the rubber in the cushions is backed against steel. This has made the bounce of the ball so much more consistent and predictable, especially in escaping snookers. If you play a shot against a cushion at, say, ten miles per hour, nowadays, it will rebound at more-or-less the same speed.

I don't want to run down the quality of today's players. The top eight in the world are far better than I ever was but the next two hundred players in the rankings have profited from the game being made easier. This has made it possible for the likes of Hendry and O'Sullivan to be knocked out in the first round of tournaments even though these greats have a level of consistency that is awesome compared with the standards set in the 80s. Short games of say nine frames make it possible for the journeyman pro to be able to win five frames in just a few visits to the table.

Snooker is still the major table game in this country. A lot of people have played pool in recent years as the table is so compact and can fit easily into most backrooms of pubs but it has failed to ignite as a professional sport in Britain. All the channels have tried it but viewing figures have been relatively disappointing. There is no national star in the game and this has been the main bar to any progress in the sport. Without a major talent, there has been little interest amongst the public and, as a result, there has been a dearth of sponsors and a lukewarm response from advertisers. As a game, it has had a difficult battle to establish itself outside of the USA in exactly the same way that American football and baseball have failed to usurp the hold of soccer and cricket on the British public. There is a major cultural hurdle in its way but I think that pool is a poor spectator sport with a limited number of playing options, strategies and situations.

Sky has had some recent success, however, with the nine ball version of the game. They promoted the Mosconi Cup in Las Vegas recently as a tournament played on Ryder Cup lines, as a team game between the USA and Europe. The audience figures were promising as this version of the game, with its small, tight pockets, is really exciting compared with the Mickey Mouse eight ball game.

The decline of the other major game, billiards, is a completely different story. In the late nineteenth century, it was the game played by the wealthy until the introduction of snooker and remained the bigger game for a long time. When I first started to play snooker, I also spent a lot of time practising billiards and, in 1970, I won the national Under-16 championship. Snooker was my main preoccupation but I continued playing billiards and retained my national championship as an Under-19 for the next three years. My billiards style was influenced by my habits in snooker as my game centred upon going for in-offs and potting the red ball three times. This snooker/billiards style is very skillful but does not make the game particularly watchable. The fundamental and inherent fault of the game is that there are only three or four shots in each game, whereas every single frame of snooker is different, with a whole plethora of ball patterns requiring many different types of shot.

I have not played billiards for nearly 15 years and will never again get the opportunity to play professionally. It still trundles on in its traditional locations, especially in India where the World Championships were held in 2003, in the city of Hyderabad. India's first World Champion in any sport was the legendary Wilson Jones who won the title in 1958 and again in 1964. With this sort of national hero, the game's future in India has been assured and reinforced by Michael Ferreira, who was champion three times, as was Geet Sethi. Apparently, there are hundreds of really talented players in India and the game attracts big enough audiences to attract television to the tournaments.

We actually have the World Champion in this country, though few people would realise this. Mike Russell won the World Championship at the tender age of 21 back in 1989 and has won the title on five subsequent occasions including 2000, 2002 and 2003. He holds the world record for the highest break under the new rules of 957 but is virtually unknown in the UK. He has a lot of skill, like all the top billiard players, and would thrash the world's top snooker players at his own game. Steve Davis played him at snooker in India in a final of the Golden Cue tournament. Mike would undoubtedly beat Steve at billiards but it was a different story in the snooker final. He managed to nick the odd frame and even managed a century break but his skills were not easily transferred to the 22 ball game and he lost heavily.

They have tried to tinker with the rules to make it more attractive. You used to be able to get the balls jammed in the pockets and make cannons and pot the red as many times as you liked. In the heyday of billiards there emerged one of sport's greatest geniuses, Walter Lindrum. He dominated the game, setting amazing records, like the break of 4,137 against Joe Davies. It took him a mind-boggling 2 hours 55 minutes to construct this break and led to the authorities changing the regulations by introducing the new baulk line rule. This had no effect on Walter, who made a break where he took the cue ball round the table to make 559 consecutive cannons. Basically, the game has not progressed. Without an icon like Lindrum, there is little chance of the game regaining its former pre-eminence.

Today's Players

Nobody has dominated snooker in the same way that Walter Lindrum dominated billiards. Joe Davis was World Champion for a long time but, in those days, World Championship tournaments were rare and Joe retained his title though a series of rather irregular challenge matches.

In the modern game, two players, Hendry and Davis, stand out not entirely for the number of world titles the pair of them have won but as great ambassadors of the sport. Steve dominated the game in the 80s, winning six titles out of eight. When a sportsman dominates a game like this, it is actually good for the sport. Motor racing gets more publicity when a genius like Michael Schumacher comes along and Davis had the same positive effect on snooker. The game was able to maintain this high profile when Steve was succeeded by Stephen Hendry, who was to dominate the game for the next decade. In the 90s, Stephen was champion a record seven times, setting an incredible benchmark for others to follow. You could argue that in the years they failed to win, the game attracted even more interest as people would look to see whether the mould had been broken. The biggest audience ever was attracted to the Davis/Taylor final of 1985 when it was estimated that over 18 million people watched the final incredible frame until well after midnight.

Steve Davis lost that final but he was the most respected player of his generation. He had those amazing powers of concentration which turned him into a great match player. Not just a great potter, he is also a great tactician. It is a testament to his mental and physical preparation that he is still in the top 16 almost a quarter of a century after he made his breakthrough in the game.

Stephen Hendry has pushed the game forward. He has developed new shots and strategies and in his peak years was the best player by a mile. He is a truly phenomenal player but doesn't have the heart of Steve Davis. The best player in the world, though he has not been World Champion since 1999, he still has the desire to win but has altered his approach to the game. He feels he can only win matches when he is scoring centuries through his outstanding break-building ability. If he is not making those hundred breaks, his game suffers. I once had a go at him in the commentary box in a match where he had won 5-4 and had scored three centuries in the process. I said that I thought he had played badly and had shown no respect for his opponent's ability. Apart from the three centuries, he had played very scrappy snooker and I felt entitled to criticise him. We had a bit of a falling out, which meant that we did not speak for a week, although he eventually conceded that I was right to pick holes in that particular performance.

Stephen is the greatest player I have ever seen. When at his best, he reaches a level no other player in the world can reach. He seems to be recapturing his old enthusiasm for the game and is, hopefully, entering a new exciting phase of his career. He seems so anxious to win, playing brilliantly, and is determined to leave an indelible mark on the game.

A measure of his greatness surfaced recently in the British Open at Brighton. He played superbly in every round, before winning the final with a series of century breaks. This was all done with a new cue after his old one was smashed in transit. I know I have gone on about this, but I really believe that it takes a great player to be able to get the feel of a brand new cue quickly. I think John Parrott taught me that lesson ...

A lot of people put Alex Higgins up amongst the greats but I think he is one of the most overrated players of all time. His 'Hurricane' style stood out as a crowd pleasing facet of his game at a time when there were a number of very meticulous, slow players in the game such as Cliff Thorburn, Terry Griffiths and, to a lesser extent, Dennis Taylor. He also built up his profile in the game through his exploits outside the playing arena but this side to his personality often masks a genuinely innovative contribution he made to the game. He developed shots that nobody knew about. His technique using the side and spinning the cue ball was different and fresh and his contribution to the development of snooker cannot be denied. But he wasn't a great player. He won the Embassy World Championship twice when he was fully focused. When he was in that frame of mind, he won matches through heart, grit and sheer determination. He looked impressive when potting and using the cushions in his flamboyant way, but he was so erratic. His cue ball control was not always of the highest standard, although he was capable of some fantastic safety play. I would never put him in the game's all-time top eight but I have got to admit that, warts and all, he made the greatest single impact of any player on snooker and helped to take it to a much wider audience.

Dennis Taylor was a complete contrast to Alex. For a long time, it looked as if Dennis was just going to be a journeyman pro. He made the best possible use of his ability and became a great match player through steady application and years of experience. His breakthrough came shortly after his mother died. He told me that he felt that she wanted him to win tournaments and he duly obliged. Dennis got to the final of the Rothman's and won the title. For a spell, he was the best player in the world, winning six tournaments in one season. He was never flashy in his stroke play and was very calm and measured, with the most remarkable ability as a safety player – just like Cliff Thorburn, who in some ways was Dennis's role model. He used to self-mockingly call himself the Son of the Grinder, but he was selling himself short.

We are great friends and I always found him a tough opponent to play. He only ever defeated me on one occasion though most matches were close. Dennis would sometimes get humpy with me and swear under his breath at me. "You lucky bastard!" was one of his favourites as he walked past me to the table but it was never said in a malicious way – I hope!

141

Dennis was one of those players like myself whose facial expression changed, almost imperceptibly, when the pressure was on. The trace of a frown would develop on his face and I could recognisable at those moments that his bottle was going. This used to happen to me and it is one of those emotions that is so hard to conceal from the television cameras and your opponent.

Dennis is a well-respected figure at tournaments. His soft Irish accent makes him very distinctive and instantly recognised as a commentator, though his knowledge of the game and his ability to analyse situations on the table are first-rate. He will always be associated with the Davis final and that amazing double-handed salute with his cue held high above his head after he sank the black. This was his iconic moment but it should not mask the simple fact that he was a great player when he was at his peak and his contribution to the game in those boom years was enormous.

John Spencer was, along with Ray Reardon, the player who dominated the years when I was a young professional. I have mentioned the inspiration he gave me when I saw him make a maximum break at a club in Manchester. He was World Champion three times (1969, 71 and 77) and was a truly great player in that era. He did not have the cue ball movement that modern top players have but he had such a great cueing action that I am sure he would have been able to adapt himself to today's game.

He would have to compete with some very talented players if he was on the circuit nowadays. One of the great players today is John Higgins. So far he has only won the World Championship once but, for me, he has taken over Steve Davis' role. He is one of the best players of all time, and is capable of a steady stream of 147s. But it is his great ability all round the table and his fantastic match playing ability that sets him aside from so many others.

Ken Doherty has similar strengths to John. Both have the strategic knowledge of the game that can help them win, even if parts of their game just aren't functioning. They can, in short, play badly to win, just as Ken did in the World Championships of 2003. He made it to the final before he was blown away by Mark Williams by playing some very mediocre snooker.

Ronnie O'Sullivan has attracted so much attention since he burst on the scene. He is the most naturally talented of all the modern players. His game can reach heights only Stephen Hendry is capable of but Ronnie's approach is inconsistent, as he himself admits, and he is struggling at present to keep his focus.

Mark Williams is the most successful player at present. He was the holder of three major championships in the same year, yet I think he has some way to go before he reaches the heights of O'Sullivan and Hendry playing at their very best. He is a great match player and is, without doubt, the best long potter the game has ever seen.

Snooker has changed over the years in which I have been involved and will continue to maintain its position as an exciting game for both participants and spectators alike. Although the heady days of the 1980s are behind us, the fact is that the game still attracts millions of television viewers, watching a new generation of talented young players compete at the highest level.